NEW PERSPECTIVES ON THE SOUTH

Charles P. Roland, General Editor

Industrialization and Southern Society 1877-1984

JAMES C. COBB

THE UNIVERSITY PRESS OF KENTUCKY

Library of Congress Cataloging in Publication Data

Cobb, James C. (James Charles), 1947-
   Industrialization and southern society, 1877-1984.

   (New perspectives on the South)
   Bibliography: p.
   Includes index.
   1. Southern States—Industries—History. 2. Indus-
trial promotion—Southern States—History. I. Title.
II. Series.
HC107.A13C64   1984   303.4'4   84-5083
ISBN 0-8131-0304-5

To Numan V. Bartley

Contents

Editor's Preface

One of the most persistent impulses in the life of the South since the Civil War has been the desire to develop an industrial economy. This urge inspired the trumpet call of such nineteenth-century New South advocates as Henry W. Grady, who, with a great deal of wishful thinking, wrote: "Surely, God has led the people of the South into this unexpected way of progress and prosperity. . . . The industrial system of the South responds, grows, thrills with new life, and it is based on sure and certain foundations. . . . [It] is built on a rock—and it cannot be shaken." The promotion of industrial growth has been a major concern of every southern state administration of the present century. World War II gave the region a vigorous push toward industrialization. At the height of that conflict the national director of the Office of War Production prophesied that within a generation the South would come to represent "the vanguard of world industrial progress." Since the war the region has indeed taken long strides in industrial expansion. Today it is being hailed, in language that sounds like Grady's, as a "Sunbelt" teeming with factories and dazzling in its prospects.

In this valuable book James C. Cobb draws upon many years of studying the history of southern industrial growth to present a balanced account of this feature of the regional experience. He weighs the principal results of this development both in causing change and in preserving continuity. By describing the relationship of southern industrial expansion to the other aspects of southern life, he makes the work highly suitable as a volume of "New Perspectives on the South." The series is designed to give a fresh and comprehensive view of the South's history as seen in the light of the striking developments since World War II. Each volume is expected to be a complete essay representing both a synthesis of the best scholarship on the subject and an interpretive analysis derived from the author's own reflections. Twenty or more volumes are planned.

CHARLES P. ROLAND

Acknowledgments

No publication project can be completed without the support and assistance of friends, family, and colleagues. This book is no exception.

Martha Doyel skillfully and cheerfully typed and retyped numerous drafts of the manuscript and never failed to provide encouragement when it was needed. Clarence L. Mohr read portions of the manuscript, as did Alexander P. Lamis. Thomas G. Dyer always managed to boost my spirits by convincing me that his work was going worse than mine.

I am indebted to all my colleagues who have made my work at the University of Mississippi and our life in Oxford so stimulating and enjoyable. Although space does not permit me to acknowledge all of those at Ole Miss who have befriended and encouraged me, I must pay tribute to Robert J. Haws, whose grasp of historiography and historical ideas has stimulated my thinking almost as often as his zest for fun and frolic have made it difficult for me to think at all.

I am particularly indebted to my family for their patience with a father and husband who too often allows his work to crowd out the most important people in his life. My son, Ben, has been exceedingly patient and good humored. I am happy that he has inherited his Dad's obsession with baseball but thankful that he did not have to depend on heredity for his skills at the game.

My wife, Lyra, remains a marvel in her ability to provide support and encouragement while maintaining an independent spirit and a sturdy skepticism of all things academic. I am grateful for her typing and editorial skills, but I would be lost without her love.

I have been especially fortunate to have been taught and advised by a consumate scholar. For the times when he mercilessly wielded his stub pencil on my dissertation and for all the times he has wielded it on my subsequent efforts, I am deeply grateful to Numan V. Bartley. Since my departure from the University of Georgia he has shared my struggle to find permanent employment and professional acceptance and has taken genuine pride in my modest accomplishments. Through it all he has treated me as his friend rather than his responsibility. I can never repay my debt to Bud Bartley but I fully acknowledge it by dedicating this book to him.

Introduction

As the contemporary South basks in the glow of national fascination with the Sunbelt it is time to explore the social, political, and institutional impact of the development of industry in Dixie. Many observers assumed that the peculiarities which set the southern states apart from the rest of the nation could survive only so long as the South remained a rural, agricultural region. Thus industrialization seemed to pose a definite threat to the distinct and often controversial qualities that gave the South its identity. Twentieth-century scholars such as James W. Silver, who questioned the future of segregation and other controversial traditions in an industrial society, operated on the premise that it was impossible "to freeze the social status quo while revolutionizing the economic order."

Those who pinned their hopes for social change on economic growth assumed that the South's experience with industrialization would parallel that of the North, where the rapid growth of industry had been accompanied by social upheaval, political realignment, and population redistribution. In the long run, however, the low-wage, labor-intensive manufacturing operations that dominated the industrializing process in the South for at least a century after the Civil War not only failed to trigger an economic revolution but proved highly adaptable to a social and political status quo that promised labor control, low taxes, and minimal government interference. Thus the South avoided a rapid social and political metamorphosis not just because its traditions were rigid but because they were also largely compatible with the type of economic growth the region had experienced during the late nineteenth century and much of the twentieth.

The quickened pace of growth in the years after World War II gave the South its long-awaited economic "take-off" replete with dynamic industries and a rapidly expanding middle class expected to lead the region's social and political transformation. The Sunbelt South did experience a number of positive changes in these areas. But even as it enjoyed its belated industrial revolution, the South remained decidedly southern, a changed society but one that still lacked many of the characteristics traditionally associated with an industrial economy. A distinctive economic and cultural heritage was partially responsible, but a close analysis reveals that most of those who studied the impact of economic development on the process did so through "northern eyes" that could see no alternative to the "classic capitalist" path to an industrial society. According to this view, underdeveloped, "backward" regions like the South were destined to experience democratization and overall societal progress as they embraced industrial capitalism. When, as in other parts of the world, this scenario failed to unfold fully in the South, the blame fell on traditionalism and cultural rigidity, and the possibility that capitalism could not only tolerate but benefit from and actually bolster a conservative, often undemocratic, social and political climate was seldom considered.

There is considerable irony in the persistent tendency to associate the South much more closely with the defense of tradition than with the pursuit of progress. In fact, industrial development became the consuming passion of regional, state, and local leaders in the Post-Reconstruction South, so much so that Marshall Frady did not overstate the case when he asserted: "In the South, the land of Canaan came to consist of a horizon of smokestacks. Industrialization—the devout acquisition of factories—became a kind of second religion there: the secular fundamentalism." As a genuine regional obsession, industrialization exerted a profound influence on policymaking and became an inescapable reality for a steadily expanding mass of southerners. The evolving economy of the New South reflected the persistent influence of the Old, an influence that also helped to perpetuate many of the social and political relationships that had been forged in the antebellum period. Hence, a fuller understanding of the history of the South since Reconstruction requires close attention to the role played by industrialization in facilitating certain changes while thwarting others.

This book synthesizes the relevant historical research, analyzes the assumptions on which that research rested, identifies the questions it asked, and pursues some of the questions it failed to ask. It also attempts to acquaint the scholar and the general reader with the overall course of southern industrial development, beginning in the antebellum era but with particular emphasis on the period since the end of Reconstruction. In addition to explaining what sorts of industries developed in the South (defined here as the Confederate South plus Kentucky and Oklahoma) this study analyzes the principal results of industrial growth in terms of influences for change and support for continuity. The sources for this volume and suggestions for further reading are identified in the Bibliographic Note which begins on page

The reader will find, perhaps, more than ample attention to such topics as planter-industrialist conflict and collusion, the evolution of the middle-class, and the repression of labor. Within the limitations of space and source material, however, this book also attempts to explore another facet of the story—that of the southerners who were caught up in the ongoing process of industrialization, the mill-hands and assembly-line workers, many of them first or second generation off-the-farm, for whom the factory became a refuge from the impoverishment, creeping or galloping, that threatened so much of southern agriculture in the twentieth century.

My own family made the transition from farming to industry in the early 1960s. Our fertile but consistently unprofitable farm had been most lucrative in the Soil Bank years when the Department of Agriculture had paid us not to farm. My father, a man already in his fifties, finally had no choice but to seek employment in a local shock absorber plant. His move into industry produced the largest and steadiest income my family had ever enjoyed.

My father's new job was not by any means an unmixed blessing, however. As a farmer he had often worked a dawn-to-sunset day during the planting and harvesting periods. Yet eight hours at an indoor, sit-down job left him drained and listless, and he so obviously dreaded his daily toil that his morning "goodbyes" to us were protracted and almost pathetic. He lived for the weekends, and his greatest source of pride was his garden, where he spent countless hours pampering the largest and sweetest cantaloupes North Georgia had ever seen.

On his tractor he had been the master of his domain. Struggling to hold a worn-out combine together he had somehow always managed to subdue his machinery until another year's grain was cut. In the factory, however, he fought a losing battle with machines that mystified and humiliated him, often to the delight of some of his younger and crueler co-workers. In retrospect, I realize that my father's experience came close to bearing out John Crowe Ransom's contention that "the dignity of personality . . . is gone as soon as the man from the farm goes in the factory door."

My father's move into industry contributed to aggregate statistics that pointed to regional economic progress. Certainly as a family we felt we were experiencing progress. Yet for my father there was an important sacrifice of both status and, unfortunately, self-respect. Granted, there was little dignity or satisfaction in the role of inadequate "provider" for one's family, but in the annual struggle against the odds, the challenge of the planting season, the satisfaction of the harvest, and the overall feeling of independence, the farm offered my father something he never found in "the plant."

The overall story of industrial growth was one of regional and individual progress, but if the pluses of the industrial experience outweighed the minuses, these minuses were far from insignificant. The sacrifices that accompanied industrial development became all too apparent in the Sunbelt era as southerners and northerners alike acknowledged that there had been more to the southern way of life than racism and demagoguery, and asked whether the South, which they had once hoped would be saved by industrialization, could now be saved from it.

1. The Shaping of Southern Growth

The antebellum South is etched indelibly into the minds of most Americans as a land of plantation agriculture where industrialists were as rare as abolitionists and nearly as unwelcome. Both mythology and historical scholarship have focused so intensively on the plantation that relatively little attention has been given to the region's industry during the period before the Civil War. The fact that manufacturing played a generally supportive but definitely subordinate role to agriculture in the Old South profoundly influenced not only the ill-fated crusade for southern political independence, but subsequent efforts to achieve economic independence as well. An examination of the factors that limited the growth of industry in the antebellum South is a prerequisite for a better understanding of the region's economic development in the period since Reconstruction.

Before the Civil War most southern industry involved the processing of agricultural products and raw materials. Flour and corn milling were the most important manufacturing activities in terms of the value of products, although lumbering operations employed more workers than any other industry. In the upper South the tobacco industry grew so rapidly that by 1860 Virginia and North Carolina alone produced more than 60 percent of the nation's processed tobacco.

Cotton mills were "natural" industrial operations in an area with an abundance of cotton, water power, and cheap labor. The most famous southern cotton mill was William Gregg's Graniteville operation, which employed 300 "pineywoods" whites, mostly women and children. Gregg practiced a paternalistic despotism toward his employees, preaching piety and requiring attendance at the school that he built in the mill village. Like his northern counterparts, however, he saw nothing wrong with long hours and low wages. Although the incomes of Gregg's employees (four to five dollars per week for men, and three to four dollars per week for women) were considerably higher than the average earnings of agricultural workers in the South, he nonetheless estimated that his labor costs were still 20 percent lower than those of his northern competitors. Coupled with the advantage of cheaper cotton, Gregg's labor savings contributed to annual profits as high as 18 percent. A number of cotton mills were built in the South during the 1840s, but not all were as successful as Gregg's.

The rise and fall of a Natchez textile mill illustrate the difficulties inherent in establishing a factory in the antebellum South. John Robinson opened the mill in 1842 and ran into one frustration after another as he struggled against the scarcity of capital, skilled labor, and machinery, and tried in vain to convince local buyers that his products were as good as those made in New England. A merchant bought him out in 1844, brought in a Yankee manager, and began a vigorous marketing campaign. After three years the second owner gave up and sold out to two mechanics, who fared no better. The mill ceased operation in 1848. Stories such as this one help to explain why even in the record crop year of 1860, the South contributed less than 7 percent of the value of the nation's manufactured cotton goods.

Although cotton mills and other processing operations predominated, the industrial economy of the Old South showed some potential for diversification. Antebellum Charleston, for example, boasted a thriving, diversified industrial mix that included iron foundries, shipyards, wagon shops, saddleries, brickyards, and numerous other enterprises in addition to its various mills and lumber plants. Region-wide, machinery, men's clothing, and sheet metals were also important products.

The South's most notable heavy industry was Richmond's Tredegar Iron Works, which produced cannon, chain, and railroad rails. Many southern buyers seemed to prefer iron products manufactured in the North, but Tredegar supplied forty locomotives for the South's railroads. The Richmond foundry was the dominant facility in a region that ranked eighth among the world's iron producers in 1860.

The antebellum South had some factories but it was hardly a threat to the industrial dominance of the northeastern or mid-Atlantic states. In 1860 the total manufacturing output of the southern states was less than that of either Pennsylvania, Massachusetts, or New York, and was only 42 percent greater than the output for Philadelphia County, Pennsylvania. When its industrial economy was compared to that of the West, the South did not fare quite so badly, but the West's manufacturing output was still nearly twice as great in 1860.

Scholars have traditionally attributed the failure of the antebellum South to industrialize more extensively to an obsession with cotton planting and the ownership of slaves. According to this interpretation, blind devotion to unprofitable single-staple plantation agriculture tied up the region's already scarce capital, while the ready availability of slave labor discouraged immigration by the free workers needed to staff manufacturing plants. The result was an economy lacking the capital, skilled labor, or markets to support significant industrialization.

In recent years economic historians have offered several important challenges to this view. First, they have shown that plantation agriculture was indeed profitable and that reliance on slave labor did not cripple the region's economy. Although southern per capita income hovered near 75 percent of the national average between 1840 and 1860, if only the white population is considered, average wealth was nearly twice as great in the South as in the Northeast. Some scholars have even calculated that the Confederacy may have been the third or fourth richest "nation" in the world in 1861. Planters held an inordinate share of the region's wealth, but the distribution of assets and income was not markedly more inequitable than that of the antebellum North, or, for that matter, most of the twentieth-century United States.

Slave property was a relatively liquid asset, and as long as cotton profits remained good, slaves were a sound investment. Although banks were less numerous in the South and most bankers preferred to see their funds invested in cotton planting or commerce, there appears to have been capital available for considerably more industrial expansion than ever occurred. Despite persistent contentions to the contrary, slaves could also be employed in industry. During the 1850s, between 160,000 and 200,000 slaves worked in southern manufacturing, and as time passed some employers, particularly in the iron industry, began to rely increasingly on skilled slave labor. With its slave work force, the South had the potential to meet the needs of most industries that required large amounts of cheap, untrained labor, and to some extent even the needs of firms requiring greater skills.

Although planters dominated the antebellum South both economically and politically, southerners who launched industrial ventures appear to have reaped considerably greater profits than those who stuck to cotton planting. For example, according to one estimate, industrialists averaged an approximate profit of 26 percent in 1860 as compared to an "acceptable" rate of return of 10 percent among planters. In fact, southern manufacturers earned profits slightly higher than the national average in both 1850 and 1860. The key to understanding the restricted size of the South's industrial sector was not the absence of viable investment opportunities but the tendency of planters and slaveholders, the region's wealthiest investors, to shun manufacturing in favor of agriculture.

If industrial enterprises promised a greater return than cotton planting, why did planters own only 12 percent of southern manufacturing stock in 1860? Some apparently feared that large-scale expansion of industry might undermine their positions of social and political dominance, and therefore they showed little enthusiasm for enterprises other than those that processed the products of the plantation or supplied its material needs. Still, except for an occasional offhand comment intended to remind industrialists that their chosen profession was a less worthy one than cotton planting, planter-oriented legislators did little to discourage the expansion of manufacturing. The reluctance of southern planters to take advantage of attractive opportunities in industry may have reflected some social or political concerns about industrialization, but the primary explanation for their indifference to industrial projects was probably a simple preference for a relatively secure investment (slaves and land) over a potentially more lucrative but also more risky one (stock in a new factory). Failure to respond to the lure of handsome profits in manufacturing seemed to confirm the stereotypical conservatism of slow-moving southerners, but in a region where slave property made average white wealth considerably greater than in the supposedly more prosperous North, the investment behavior of southern planters was far more rational than the dogged persistence of farmers who in the 1980s still cling to a profession that they maintain is consistently unprofitable.

As long as cotton prices remained high, the dominance of the plantation system did not cripple the South's economy, but it did profoundly influence the type of industries that developed in the region. In addition to cotton mills and other similar facilities, typical antebellum factories produced cheap, rough shoes and clothing for slaves, as well as other plantation necessities such as stoves, cooking utensils, and rudimentary tools. There was little in the pattern of southern expansion to create the urban markets available in the Middle Atlantic states or the Northeast. Despite relatively high wages for certain craftsmen, most jobs in southern industry required little in the way of skill or training. Thus the region attracted relatively few inmigrants compared to the dynamic North, whose faster-growing manufacturing sector provided considerably greater opportunities. Established commercial linkages, wherein southerners bought and borrowed from and sold through northern financiers and businessmen, left the South without a strong entrepreneurial class inclined to lead the region toward economic diversification.

In their analysis of the failure of industrialization in southern slave society, Fred Bateman and Thomas Weiss warned against underestimating the antebellum South's industry or its prospects for further industrial development. They further argued that had planters been more willing to invest in manufactures the South's industrial base might have been larger. On the other hand, they also concluded that:

Even if investors had seized quickly upon industrial opportunities, if risk were not a factor, if all hesitant planters had ignored their neighbor's scorn, and if the socially conscious had considered only their private gains, the South might still have seemed under-industrialized to outside observers. The region's factor endowment would still have led to an industrial sector that was small relative to that in the East. Our evidence indicates that the region's comparative advantage [in agriculture] had been overindulged. Had this been corrected according to the prevailing market signals, the southern economic condition would have improved. But the Old South still may have had its "deplorable scarcity" in industry.

By pointing to the significant limitations on industrialization in the Old South, Bateman and Weiss suggested the extent to which the late nineteenth-century "New South" crusade for industrial development would be influenced by the economic heritage of the antebellum era. The Civil War dealt a severe blow to southern agriculture, but industry, which benefited from expanded wartime markets and managed to keep its labor force more or less intact, rebounded from the conflict relatively quickly. All the generally accepted measures of manufacturing productivity exceeded prewar levels by 1869. Between 1869 and 1899 value of output and value added by manufacturing rose more than sixfold while capital investment increased more than ten times.

Southern manufacturing showed consistent growth throughout the nineteenth century, but the growth of Dixie's industry seemed less impressive when viewed against the backdrop of rapid industrial expansion elsewhere in the nation. Between 1850 and 1880 an already deficient South lost ground dramatically in every major category of industrial vitality when compared to the United States as a whole.

Given the relatively small industrial base with which the South entered the postbellum era, southern industry could hardly have been expected to provide immediate salvation. Yet the fragile, diminutive character of southern industry also impeded the modernization of the dominant agricultural sector, which failed to move significantly beyond prewar productivity levels. The rate of growth in the per capita crop output of the major cotton producing states fell in each of the last three decades of the nineteenth century and slowed to an almost negligible pace in the 1890s.

Coupled with a decline in world demand for cotton, which grew at an average annual rate of 5 percent between 1820 and 1860 but at only 1.3 percent between 1866 and 1895, the stagnation of productivity made the absence of a viable industrial sector all the more crucial. The exploitive nature of the sharecropping and mercantile systems reduced the incomes of individual farmers to near subsistence level, denying them the capital to invest in increased productivity and discouraging them from taking the risks involved in attempting to achieve a measure of self-sufficiency by growing more of their own food. In the absence of a manufacturing component sufficient to stimulate demand for agricultural diversification (greater production of foodstuffs for industrial workers) or to generate the competition for labor and the investment capital needed to spur productivity, agriculture could only be as viable as the generally unfavorable late nineteenth-century market conditions permitted. Capital-starved and technologically laggard, southern agriculture and southern industry remained locked in a mutually dependent relationship in which the weaknesses of one reinforced the weaknesses of the other.

At the end of Reconstruction the South seemed to have little hope for rapid economic growth, but the proponents of industrialization were not easily discouraged. One of the first prominent southerners to take on the challenge of stimulating economic progress in the immediate post-Civil War period was J.D.B. Debow, who had been a tireless advocate of industrialism in the antebellum years. More than many of his New South successors, Debow recognized the obstacles posed by the region's lack of capital, skilled labor, and markets, but he was nonetheless certain that manufacturing represented the South's "true remedy": "We have got to go to manufacturing to save ourselves. We have got to go to it to obtain an increase of population. Workmen go to furnaces, mines, and factories—they go where labor is brought. Every new furnace or factory is sure to come from the neighborhood or from abroad. Capital, to the extent that the South shall have occasion to borrow, will, by law of economy that never fails, flow here to erect, equip and start every manufacturing establishment as fast as it can profitably be run."

Optimistic as it was, Debow's urgent call for industrialization paled in comparison to the hyperbole of the New South prophets who followed him. Promising prosperity and economic independence through industrialization, the principal New South spokesmen were an interesting but perplexing lot. Former Pennsylvanian William D. "Pig Iron" Kelly was also a former Radical Republican. Publisher Richard Edmonds crammed his *Manufacturers' Record* with questionable statistics to support an unbridled optimism concerning the South's industrial future. Daniel Augustus Tompkins, a frequent contributor to Edmonds's publication, even dared to correct Thomas Jefferson, matter-of-factly asserting that Jefferson's vision of an agrarian utopia had led the South temporarily off course in its journey toward industrial prosperity.

The most famous New South prophet was Henry W. Grady, the son of an Athens, Georgia, businessman, who after several unsuccessful publishing ventures became editor of the influential *Atlanta Constitution*. Throughout the late 1880s Grady tirelessly championed the cause of industrial growth in the columns of the most widely read paper in Dixie, but he was to gain far greater fame for what he said than for what he wrote. Though not always logical, the silver-tongued Grady was always persuasive as he enumerated the South's seemingly limitless possibilities for industrial development.

In an effort to underscore these possibilities Grady revived and modified a parable that had been used by antebellum advocates of industrialization and presented it as an account of a funeral he had attended in Pickens County, Georgia:

> They buried him in the midst of a marble quarry; they cut through solid marble to make his grave; and yet a little tombstone they put above him was from Vermont. They buried him in the heart of a pine forest, and yet the pine coffin was imported from Cincinnati. They buried him within touch of an iron mine, and yet the nails in his coffin and the iron in the shovel that dug the grave were imported from Pittsburgh. They buried him by the side of the best sheep-grazing country on the earth, and yet the wool in the coffin bands and the coffin bands themselves were brought from the North. The South didn't furnish a thing on earth for that funeral but the corpse and the hole in the ground.

Realizing that the South's best hope for industrial capital lay with northern financiers, Grady deemphasized sectional animosity and professed his region's desire to let bygones be bygones. He delivered his most famous oration before the New England Society of New York at Delmonico's Restaurant in 1886. An audience dominated by wealthy businessmen waited impatiently through a brief address by the South's old nemesis, William Tecumseh Sherman. As the last strains of "Marching through Georgia" faded away, an undaunted Grady rose to tell the crowd what it wanted to hear: "There was a South of slavery and secession—that South is dead. There is a South of union and freedom—that South, thank God, is living, breathing, growing every hour." To affirm this bold assertion, Grady took it upon himself to anoint Abraham Lincoln as the personification of national unity, a man whose character combined the best attributes of both the Puritan and the Cavalier. To further show his region's good faith, Grady practically thanked General Sherman for burning Atlanta, whose ashes had given rise to "a brave and beautiful city," built like the rest of the New South without "one ignoble prejudice or memory."

Seeing that this last and most audacious assertion had won an emotional acceptance, Grady painted an attractive portrait of a resurrected region awaiting the investments of the North's captains of industry: "We have smoothed the path to Southward, wiped out where the Mason and Dixon's line used to be, and hung out our latchstring to you and yours." Although Grady was willing to erase the Mason-Dixon line, he offered no apologies for what or where the South had been. In fact, the role of the Old South in the rhetoric of the New was to become one of the most paradoxical aspects of the crusade to bring industrial prosperity to the region. Advocates of industrial development promised a prosperous New South based on economic modernization, but they were also careful to pay homage to a mythical "Gone with the Wind" vision of an antebellum society peopled by aristocratic beaux and belles who lived in elegant white-columned mansions surrounded by fragrant magnolias. This posthumous celebration of a nonindustrial, noncapitalistic society went hand-in-hand with tributes to the Lost Cause and the use of Confederate heroes to boost the crusade for economic expansion. A ghostly antebellum planter became the cartoonist's symbol for the New South crusade.

While repeated tributes to the Lost Cause may have been counterproductive in terms of the efforts of New South leaders to encourage sectional reconciliation, the glorification of the Old South was at least in part a psychological device, designed to help humiliated southerners hold their heads up as they accepted much-needed investment capital from their Yankee conquerors. The homage paid the region's past was an ego-soothing balm for despondent ex-Confederates who needed reassurance that their cause, though lost, was not forgotten. Ironically, as depicted in the rhetoric and literature of the New South, the Old South also became an attractive bit of mythology to nonsoutherners, perhaps because the Dixie of magnolias and moonlight provided such a pleasing contrast to the crass acquisitiveness of northern industrial society in the "Gilded Age" of the late nineteenth century. At any rate, as northern investors moved to take advantage of the opportunities described by New South hucksters, popular novels embraced the cause of reunion (and economic cooperation) by featuring romantic encounters between southern belles and their Yankee suitors. Presumably these relationships, like the marriage of northern capital and southern labor, were destined to produce years of happiness and satisfaction for both the fortunate participants.

A century after the emergence of the New South crusade, historians have yet to reach a consensus on its goals or its role in shaping the economy and society of the post-Reconstruction South. Were the apostles of industrial development really seeking a "New" South or did they merely hope to graft a restrictive, exploitive industrial component onto an economic and social structure roosted in the region's plantation past? One school of thought has New South leaders representing an ascendant middle class threatening to break the grip of wealthy landowners on the levers of economic and political influence in the region. According to C. Vann Woodward, spokesmen for the movement were "more than advocates of industrialism," they were preaching "a new philosophy and way of life and a new scale of values."

A more skeptical interpretation holds that the New South movement represented a shift in neither direction nor leadership but became instead a force for continuity by insuring that conservative planters would play a crucial role in shaping the region's industrial development. Thus observers such as Wilbur J. Cash and more recently Jonathan Wiener and Dwight B. Billings, Jr., have contended that the New South movement's commitment to the plantation ideal was not mere propaganda but in fact represented a capitulation by New South leaders to the dominant influence of planters unwilling to surrender control of the region's destiny to an emergent industrial middle class.

In their respective studies of late nineteenth-century North Carolina and Alabama, Billings and Wiener argued that a coalition of planters and industrialists acted to insure that the New South would be constructed on a plantation foundation. Some advocates of industrialization had spoken initially of a balanced economy wherein independently owned, diversified farms would feed predominantly industrial urban centers. In the face of planter reluctance to yield power, and the threat of political and social upheaval posed by the agrarian movements of the 1880s and 1890s, however, New South spokesmen recognized the special interests of affluent landholders and gave their assurances that industrial development would not undermine the sharecropping system by siphoning away surplus labor. Nor would it engender class consciousness and thereby threaten the stability essential not only to planter hegemony but to the attraction of investment capital.

Wiener contended that a conservative coalition of planter and manufacturing interests had led Alabama down the "Prussian Road" to industrial expansion. Billings found a similar pattern of "conservative modernization" in North Carolina, whose economic development he compared to that of Japan and Germany in the nineteenth century. In both states the social and political structures remained agrarian-oriented, and manufacturing growth centered on low-wage, labor-intensive industries, most of which were involved in processing raw materials or agricultural products. Wiener and Billings found that the New South of the late nineteenth century remained a closed society, heavily influenced if not dominated by conservative planters but nonetheless offering industrial investors a relatively free hand to exploit the region's human and natural resources.

Like Cash, Wiener and Billings laid much of the responsibility for the economic, political, and social continuity between the Old and New South at the doorstep of the planter. Although planters played an important role in shaping late nineteenth-century society, their influence on the evolution of industry in that period may have been less significant than the economic heritage forged by their antebellum predecessors. Would-be promoters of industrial development had little choice but to defer to the potent legacy of single-staple agriculture. In *The Political Economy of the Cotton South,* Gavin Wright argued that the end of the antebellum cotton boom had changed the South from "a society fundamentally organized around labor scarcity into a classic prototype of a labor surplus region." According to Wright, the best opportunities for altering the South's economic future were lost in the antebellum period "when cotton prosperity did not generate strong nonagricultural skills and activity." "Given this legacy," Wright concluded, "it is doubtful that the choices open to the postbellum South could have made much difference for the region as a whole."

New South spokesmen inherited economic leadership of a region likely to attract only low-paying, labor- and resource-exploitive manufacturing operations. Like their counterparts in other less developed areas, they realized that their states were in no position to compete for industries other than those that could take advantage of an ample supply of unskilled but dirt-cheap labor and abundant natural resources. Executives of such industries were just as interested in maintaining social and political stability, low taxes, inexpensive labor, and minimal, conservative government as were the South's politically powerful planters. The promises of continuity offered by New South spokesmen reflected not only enduring planter influence but the desires of those who would manage the region's new factories and commercial enterprises.

The New South's industrial investors seldom objected to the plantation style of government and politics, and showed little if any interest in providing significant upward mobility for low-income whites. Certainly the process of industrialization posed no serious threat to a system of caste that condemned black southerners to socioeconomic and political deprivation. Tensions over potential competition for labor were always present, but the desire of most industrial employers to keep wages as low as possible, and a locational pattern that kept factories out or at least at the edge of the plantation belt, kept such antagonism to a minimum. The plantation society of the New South accommodated itself to industrialization so well because the South was attracting labor- and resource-oriented "plantation industries" whose executives and managers joined the region's planters in the practice of what Harold D. Wood-man called "unfettered capitalism," free from the restraints imposed elsewhere by growing labor militance and the threat of increased government regulation. In the long run it was not only the strength of conservative planter influences but the compatibility of these influences with the goals and preferences of the region's industrialists that kept the plantation at the center of the New South's political and economic order.

The persistence of the antebellum pattern of dependence on labor-intensive, extractive, and processing operations shaped the industrial economy of the New South. The late nineteenth and early twentieth centuries witnessed the expansion of textile, tobacco, lumber, and other industries to which a southern location offered ample low-cost labor and proximity to the agricultural and natural resources they processed. The industries that grew most rapidly in the post-Reconstruction decades were typical of an underdeveloped economy in that they utilized both cheap labor and abundant raw materials. Cotton processing industries chose Piedmont locations, Texas and Louisiana attracted petroleum and sulphur refining facilities, while Kentucky, Alabama, and Virginia contributed significant amounts of coal. By 1900 southern forests were providing nearly one-third of the nation's raw timber. As vital as they were to the New South's economy, such industries hardly promised to elevate the region to economic parity with the rest of the nation.

Late nineteenth-century Georgia presented a clear picture of the industrial base of the New South. Georgia towns had responded to the call to "Get out and get yourselves a cotton mill," and the state boasted fifty-three such mills in 1890. The lumber and naval stores industries grew significantly during the 1880s, as did other extractive, processing-oriented operations such as flour and grist mills, tanneries, distilleries, and brickyards. Two more agriculture-related industries, fertilizer and cotton seed oil, flourished in the 1880s. In 1884 both bakeries and distilleries showed an aggregate output valued in excess of $1 million.

At the end of the nineteenth century, grist and flour milling accounted for more than 20 percent of Tennessee's industrial production. Nashville was the flour milling center but Knoxville and Memphis also had their share of mills. In fact, with corn, wheat, and water power readily available, a number of small towns had grist or flour mills. The timber industry was also important in Tennessee. Memphis was the largest inland supplier of hardwood in the world. Across the state iron and steel employed nearly 2,000 workers, and textiles, cotton, and tobacco processing plants were proliferating.

In its locational requirements and economic impact, the textile industry was typically southern. The southward migration of textile mills began in earnest in the 1890s, and by 1904 southern mills used more cotton and produced more yarn than those of New England. Still, the expansion of the textile industry did not spark the rapid economic growth that New South boosters predicted. Longer hours and lower wages remained the major incentives to textile investment in the South. Innovations in production technology were more or less complete by 1900, and textile mills had little need for more skilled, better paid labor after that time. Consequently, the region's pool of textile workers held no attraction for other industries seeking markets or a more accomplished labor force.

Textile expansion did little to facilitate rapid population concentration, especially after 1900, when the proliferation of electric power made it possible for the industry to disperse in small plants located in labor-surplus rural areas. These plants were generally too small to produce the finished, higher quality products that would have meant greater profits and faster expansion. Because so many of its workers remained rural and small-town residents who grew much of their own food, the southern textile industry provided little incentive for diversification of southern agriculture.

All too often the profits from textile and other southern manufacturing, which might have supplied investment capital for other industrial ventures, were siphoned away by absentee owners, who had little stake in the region's long-term economic, social, and political future. Before the Civil War many southern leaders charged that Dixie was no more than a colony of the North. New South advocates promised to bring economic independence, and southern investors played a major role in early post-Reconstruction textile expansion. Within a short time, however, northern entrepreneurs were supplying capital, and New England operations were responding to heightened competition by moving down to take advantage of the South's cheap labor.

Northern capital played a major role in the growth of Birmingham, which sprang from a cornfield to become the center of a southern iron industry that increased its share of national production from one-sixteenth in 1880 to one-tenth in 1890. At the turn of the century the Birmingham area boasted 282 manufacturing plants whose products were valued at more than $12 million. The city bristled with coke ovens, iron foundries, and rolling mills; but its plants also produced a number of non-iron-related products.

The Alabama iron industry benefited from the rapid expansion of the region's railroads, which grew about 20 percent faster than the national average in the 1880s. Railroad growth was spurred by the infusion of northern capital, a general trend toward consolidation, and the decision to adjust track width to a northern standard. When the Louisville and Nashville line connected to the Alabama and Chattanooga near Birmingham, the company invested in local ventures, offered discount fares to potential investors, and provided special rates for pig iron produced in the area. By 1900 Birmingham's products were flowing north on eight lines serving the city.

The expansion of the Alabama iron industry was accompanied by considerable boosterism and profiteering. Iron production rose from 203,000 tons in 1885 to over 915,000 tons in 1892, as blast furnaces flourished, often encouraging the development of new towns seemingly destined to become industrial centers. Promoters painted vivid portraits of future prosperity, describing Fort Payne as "The New England City of the South," Gadsden as "The Hub of the Mineral Belt," and Tuscaloosa as "Alabama's Natural Pittsburg."

Backers of these "blast furnace" towns purchased large land options and hastily laid out a village, often constructing only a grand hotel and perhaps a bank for the benefit of would-be investors. If not actually erected, a blast furnace was certainly promised, along with rolling mills, coke ovens, and all the operations associated with the iron boom. Promotional pamphlets provided glowing assessments of local resources, even if considerable evidence existed to the contrary. First purchasers were often members of the development company who bid astronomical but fictitious sums for choice lots in order to trigger a "bandwagon" effect among other bidders. Such promotional endeavors peaked at the end of the 1880s before falling victim to the Panic of 1893 and a saturated pig iron market.

By the mid-1890s many of the once-heralded industrial metropolises such as Gadsden, Fort Payne, and Anniston had seen furnaces close, land sales fizzle, and their opportunistic boosters move on to areas with more attractive prospects.

The corporate failures accompanying the Panic of 1893 ultimately expanded northern influence on the South's industrial economy. In 1907 when J. P. Morgan secured President Theodore Roosevelt's blessing for United States Steel's purchase of the Tennessee Coal and Iron Company, Birmingham's boosters hailed the takeover of local operations as a giant step forward. Optimists promised a prosperous future, but company officials had no intention of allowing their newly acquired operations to compete with their established northern ones. Under United States Steel's "Pittsburgh Plus" system, all iron or steel shipped from Birmingham had to be sold at a price equal to the price of steel sold by the company at Pittsburgh plus the freight rates from Pittsburgh, regardless of the buyer's location. Moreover, instead of supplying the higher-priced and more profitable kinds of steel, the Birmingham forges were restricted to the production of cruder pig, sheet, and bar iron.

"Pittsburgh Plus" not only gave steel consumers an incentive to locate in Pennsylvania rather than Alabama, but it stunted the growth of Birmingham's market area. Birmingham's products were seldom seen in many parts of the South. One estimate suggested that the Alabama iron center's output would have been 250 percent larger had its ties to southern customers not been curtailed by "Pittsburgh Plus." Largely as a result of U.S. Steel's efforts to control production and marketing of Birmingham's steel, the South's proportion of national steel production fell by 50 percent between 1893 and 1913.

Birmingham's experience illustrated the colonial nature of much late nineteenth-century southern industrial development, but most local leaders were more than happy to have their communities exploited by absentee investors. For example, northern capital and expertise were vital to Chattanooga's economic expansion, as the Chattanooga *Daily Times* noted in a syrupy attempt at symbolism in 1883: "The frozen fingers of the North have been laid in the warm palms of the South, and a healthful, invigorating temperature pervades them both as one body."

In the minds of the small-town elite a cotton mill represented the first step toward industrial vitality. A mania for mills followed the Atlanta International Cotton Exposition in 1881, as evidenced by the assertion of the preacher who declared that "Next to God, what this town needs most is a cotton mill." Proud boosters were always happy to supply visitors with the dimensions of the local smokestack and explain that the regular blasts from the mill's whistles provided the entire county with its time standard. The quest of Raleigh, North Carolina, for such a mill was spurred on by the fact that "Wilmington has one, Charlotte is thinking about establishing one, and Raleigh should not be behind the times." The Raleigh editor who championed the cotton mill cause had doubtless observed the growth which textile mills had brought to Charlotte, Gastonia, Greensboro, and other towns at the end of the nineteenth century. After Raleigh's newly organized Chamber of Commerce succeeded in laying the groundwork for a mill that opened in 1890, the city soon attracted leather, wagon, and cider and vinegar manufacturers, to name but a few. A now happy local editor assured his readers: "It is absolutely certain that Raleigh is destined to be a large and important manufacturing centre."

Since Broadus Mitchell's 1921 study citing philanthropy as one of the motives for mill building, there has been considerable disagreement as to whether the mill movement was based entirely on the profit motive or derived in part from a humanitarian concern for Dixie's poor whites. As David Carlton has pointed out, the movement was probably more philanthropic at the community than at the individual or class level. The founder or founders of a cotton mill provided a community with jobs for the idle, payrolls to be spent at local stores, and the general social, civic, and religious benefits that were held to accompany economic progress. Rather than mutually exclusive, the goals of profit and philanthropy were dependent and compatible.

The move to establish textile mills in the inland towns of South Carolina was dominated by the business and professional elements, who viewed their town as a corporate enterprise in which they held stock. Therefore they should oversee its governance. On the other hand, efforts to involve local farmers in mill promotion ran headlong into the traditional problem of capital scarcity. For example, an Abbeville, South Carolina, farmer proclaimed his dedication to the cotton mill cause by boldly declaring his willingness to contribute twenty or perhaps even forty dollars. Seldom able to raise the necessary funds locally, would-be mill builders had little choice but to court northern investors.

Throughout the late nineteenth century fierce competition for new industry contributed to rising and falling fortunes across the urban South. Richmond lost its leadership as an iron production center to Birmingham and its preeminence in tobacco to the North Carolina tobacco-belt towns of Winston and Durham. Memphis staked its future on cotton and became the nation's leading supplier of cotton seed oil.

Manufacturing also accelerated the growth of the small-town South. The growth of Laurel, Mississippi, was almost wholly attributable to the expansion of the timber industry. The population of Laurel swelled from 3,313 in 1870 to nearly 30,000 in 1910 as the city's lumber mills shipped yellow pine all over the nation and the world. Land values climbed rapidly and local business boomed. By 1915, as the leading lumber producer in the state, Laurel was the envy of the other growth-conscious Mississippi communities.

Despite gains in manufacturing, at the turn of the century the urban South's economy remained predominantly commercial, centering on trade with the countryside. Employment in urban manufacturing lagged well behind the average for the nation's largest cities, the South's cities remaining more dependent on transportation and services to provide jobs for their residents. Even a relatively manufacturing-oriented city such as Memphis was linked closely to its hinterland. At the turn of the century Memphis produced manufactured goods worth $18 million, but as the region's premier cotton market the city's annual trade stood at $200 million. The economic supremacy of commerce put business and professional leaders in a position to sponsor and also to shape their city's industrial growth. The dominance of commerce in the urban South manifested itself in a pattern of political leadership. Merchants figured prominently in southern city politics long after industrialists had risen to the top in the North, and even when industrialists did join the urban power elite the changes were hardly noticeable. David Goldfield explained that "industrialists usually possessed the same values as merchants (frequently they were former merchants), especially if they engaged in some aspect of staple crop processing."

As in colonial Latin America, the New South's middle class had a vested interest in exporting the raw materials of a countryside to which it, in turn, distributed manufactured products imported from outside the region. As Numan Bartley observed, "The prosperity of urban merchants—and indeed the prosperity of towns and cities themselves—were deeply enmeshed in existing economic arrangements."

"Existing economic arrangements" hardly translated into prosperity for the South's small farmers, whose fear of slipping into tenancy intensified their frustrations with high interest rates, tight credit, and local banking and mercantile monopolies, and helped to spur them into political revolt in the 1880s and 90s. By the formation of cooperatives and the advocacy of a "subtreasury" program wherein crops would serve as collateral for federally funded loans, the Farmer's Alliance and its heir, the Populist Party, threatened, in Bartley's words, "to shift the center of economic gravity from Wall Street to the agricultural provinces." Calls for increased government regulation of industry and commerce pursued a similar goal, but for southern conservatives the greatest threat posed by these movements was an appeal to black voters, an appeal that opponents warned would surely divide whites and quickly undermine their overall supremacy.

Few of the white agrarian insurgents envisioned a racially egalitarian South, but they did challenge the prevailing hierarchy within white society. In the long run their efforts probably drew the small-town merchant/professional classes even closer to the planters by using them as scapegoats in order to bring the dirt farmers together. Merchants, bankers, and lawyers were pointedly excluded from Alliance membership in some states. Even when an agrarian spokesman such as Tom Watson made an appeal for the support of the region's mercantile class, his tone was threatening: "Tell me, Mr. Merchant, if you destroy the prosperity of my farm where will you get your customers?" In the long run any effort by the Alliance or the Populists to recruit the region's dependent middle class was doomed to fail for it asked merchants and professionals to sever their economic ties at both ends—with the northern manufacturer whose goods were distributed by the southern middle class, and with the planter who bought these products and grew the crops whose export was also vital to the survival of the region's businessmen. Faced with a challenge to their immediate best interests and uncertain about their own future in the more open society the insurgents envisioned, the South's commercial middle class maintained its fidelity to the planters.

The turn-of-the-century South was home to many more manufacturing establishments than the South of 1865, but the gains of the late nineteenth century had done relatively little to narrow the economic gap between the region and the rest of the United States. With nearly 30 percent of the nation's population, the southern states produced only 10 percent of its nonagricultural income. In 1910, Georgia's manufacturing payroll was still smaller than Cincinnati's. Meanwhile, 82 percent of Dixie's work force was still employed in farm-related pursuits. Instead of gaining ground, the South had managed only to maintain per capita personal income at 51 percent of the national average between 1880 and 1900.

The industrial growth of the late nineteenth and early twentieth centuries followed a self-perpetuating pattern. The appeal to low-wage, labor-intensive industries entailed a commitment to maintaining the economic and governmental conditions desired by the management of such industries. Wages had to be held down by suppressing unionization efforts and by maintaining a surplus of workers grateful for any kind of industrial employment. No industry likely to accept unionization or pay higher than prevailing wage scales could be recruited. Southern political and economic leaders felt they had little choice, given the underdeveloped state of the South's economy, but to give industrialists and industrial development advocates whatever they wanted.

Although the New South experienced economic progress it never fully overcame the handicaps that had retarded the expansion of industry in the Old South. Absentee ownership drew away the profits that might have become investment capital, and low wages prevented the accumulation of buying power needed to provide an attractive, growth-accelerating consumer market. With 90 percent of the region's railroad mileage owned by northerners, at the turn of the century southern shippers faced freight rate discrimination so severe that the cost of sending cotton from Little Rock to Columbia was 21 cents per 100 pounds higher than the cost of moving it from Little Rock to Fall River, Massachusetts, a distance approximately twice as great.

Ironically, the expansion of the southern railway system shaped the region's urban development by further diminishing the prospects for a large number of cities likely to support major industries. Excellent connections to northern markets enabled "crossroads" merchants to market local crops without transshipment to major cities. In turn, the products of the manufacturing North were also directly accessible to the country merchant, whose business flourished in proportion to the stagnation of many regional cities. Processing towns grew up in the cotton belt, but they seldom grew beyond 10,000 in population because their market areas were limited and the basic processing of cotton required neither a concentration of technology nor skilled labor.

The tendency of southern industries to locate in rural areas in order to draw on a surplus of agricultural labor also discouraged the rapid urbanization that might have attracted more market-oriented industries. North Carolina led the South in manufacturing employment in 1900, but its population remained more than 90 percent rural. Only 13.5 percent of southerners were urbanites at the turn of the century as compared to over 30 percent of midwesterners and nearly 60 percent of northeasterners.

The region's experience in the last quarter of the nineteenth century supported Gavin Wright's argument that the postbellum South had relatively few choices as to the course of its future economic development. The cotton-centered agricultural economy required relatively little in the way of supporting industrial activities similar to those that developed in the more agriculturally diverse Midwest and Northeast. The South's labor pool and its abundant raw materials were its major assets in the struggle to industrialize, but untrained workers, water, and wood were no substitute for skilled workers, coal, and iron when it came to attracting capital and entrepreneurship in a rapidly modernizing national industrial economy.

Surveying the South's dilemma in the late nineteenth century, William N. Parker argued that the region's problem "did not lie in exploitation, a skewed income distribution, or a drain of agricultural profits to the North. In effect, the South's growth path in 1866 could hardly have occurred otherwise except as part of a national economic and social policy which would have redistributed labor and capital within the nation, . . . without regard to race, locality or previous social structure." Such a policy, Parker noted, was beyond even the scope of the New Deal of the 1930s, and therefore unthinkable in the late nineteenth century, an "era of laissez faire and the growth of the large, private corporation."

As both Parker and Wright indicated, the decisions that shaped the economy of the New South were made in the Old South. Moreover, it is by no means certain that even if the antebellum years had produced greater interest in industrialization, the New South would have developed a manufacturing sector in any way comparable to that of the North. The argument that a more democratic, progressive social and political philosophy would have facilitated a more rapid rate of growth ignored the primacy of such economic factors as resources, labor, and markets that made and kept southern industry what and where it was. The South entered the twentieth century with an economy that remained predominantly agricultural. Industry was more important to that economy than it had been forty years earlier, but the plantation still towered above the factory, shaping it and most of the rest of southern society in its own image.

2. The Twentieth-Century South and the Campaign for New Industry

Although the emerging pattern of industrial development seemed largely compatible with the post-bellum South's social and political hierarchy, a sizable industrial sector could not be created within a fundamentally agricultural society without engendering significant tensions. The agrarian uprisings of the 1880s and 1890s had posed enough of a threat to the region's racial and class hierarchy to encourage the disfranchisement of most of its blacks and a good number of its lower-class whites. Even so, the creation of a white industrial working class, often laboring and living in unhealthy, frustrating, and degrading conditions, could not but raise concerns about the future unity of white society. Hence the Progressive reforms of the early twentieth century aimed not only at "uplift" but at control of the white masses. Meanwhile, in the South, as in the nation at large, Progressive improvements in transportation, governmental modernization, and modest efforts at regulation of industry and commerce promised a more efficient, unified society capable of absorbing progress without surrendering its stability. Southern Progressivism, particularly the Business Progressivism of the 1920s, fused the reform impulse and the concept of expanded state responsibility with the campaign for industrial growth to spawn an era of state-sponsored recruitment of new industry.

With industry still growing slowly, merchants and professionals in the early twentieth-century South retained strong ties to agriculture, and thus offered no significant challenge to the region's planter class. So long as a large segment of the South's middle class could secure a worthwhile income as small-town lawyers, bankers, or merchants who serviced and supplied local farms, they accepted a political status quo that reflected the dominant position of agriculture in the region's economy.

Such circumstances hardly seemed to provide a fertile climate for a reform movement, especially one that most scholars have described as an urban crusade aimed at extending public services to support economic development and a more comfortable and satisfying lifestyle for the middle class. Innovations such as improved streets and other facilities, as well as measures aimed at making government more efficient and businesslike, seemed largely urban-oriented, but the willingness of the rural and small-town agricultural/professional/commercial/industrial elite to embrace or at least tolerate these and other Progressive reforms stemmed from the fact that these changes often benefited and seldom threatened this group's interests. First, the specter of challenge from below had been dispelled by the disfranchisement laws which created a safer, more controllable body politic likely to embrace the reforms espoused by Progressive spokesmen without being tempted to flirt with more fundamental structural changes that might alter traditional power relationships. Efforts to improve roads clearly helped planters, merchants, and small-town manufacturers, as did attempts to regulate railroads or fertilizer producers whose excesses had proven harmful to the region's agriculturally oriented commercial and industrial economy. Progressive improvements in education, felt largely in the white schools, promised a pool of better trained, more thoroughly indoctrinated, and therefore obedient industrial laborers, while advances in public health also contributed to a more dependable and productive work force.

In actual practice much of Progressive reform had the effect of widening disparities between the South's "haves" and "have nots." Local option provisions and procedural informality gave officials considerable latitude in the collection and disbursement of revenue. Black schools often suffered because of increased support for white ones. Schools in small-farm, poor-white counties were similarly, though less drastically, disadvantaged. In Mississippi, for example, educational funds were distributed according to the number of educable children in an area, the result being that black-belt whites enjoyed a windfall because rural blacks were seldom able to send their children to school. Schools in such areas stayed open longer and paid teachers better than their counterparts in poor-white hill counties. In Georgia a similar discrepancy existed in favor of city and town schools, as opposed to rural ones, as a result of a 1904 constitutional amendment allowing localities to create their own separate school districts. In North Carolina a regressive tax structure increased the economic burden of education in the poor-white and black counties least able to shoulder it.

Although it had both a humanitarian and a moral impetus, Progressivism also reflected a concern for order in a society seeking to graft a new industrial component onto an agriculture-dominated social and political structure. In South Carolina Progressive reform aimed at insuring stability and social control in an industrializing state. With cotton mill workers becoming a distinctive, alienated class, reformers recognized that the "mill problem" was a potential threat to the unity of South Carolina whites. Thus they concentrated not only on coercing mill management to provide better working and living conditions for their workers but on "uplift" of the workers themselves. This was to be accomplished primarily through a compulsory education law and child labor reform, the goal being to replace the fiercely individualistic, "primitive" heritage of mill workers and the negative influences of the mill and mill village environment with the stabilizing, enlightened, homogenizing influence of public education. Reformers hoped that subsequent generations of mill workers would be able to shed the stigma of the mill and be assimilated into a united white society.

Ironically, the mill workers themselves often resented such reforms, seeing them as a threat to family income and as evidence of the condescension with which they were viewed by other whites. In the short run, worker resistance to Progressive "uplift" amounted to little, but historian David Carlton has linked resentment of these programs to "Bleaseism," a dramatic display of mill worker support for Coleman L. Blease, a demagogic politician who became governor of South Carolina and a dominant force in state politics between 1910 and 1917. Blease owed much of his strength to the mill workers, who saw him as their champion in a rearguard action against further encroachments by the "better element" town folk who had forced "uplift" down their throats.

In the final analysis, much of southern Progressivism may well have been conceptualized and articulated by urban spokesmen, but most reform provisions would not have seen the light of day without the assent of small-town and county-seat elites who consented to their implementation. If such leaders rarely championed Progressive measures, they also infrequently opposed them unless a specific measure threatened the wealth and power of the planter or commercial/industrial/professional classes. Because of their preeminence in the power structures where the decisions concerning the impact of new programs and policies were made, this influential elite found much to like and little to fear in the new measures.

Although atypical in some ways, Mississippi's Progressivism reflected many of the characteristics of the movement throughout the South. As Charles G. Hamilton noted: "Mississippi reformers were genuinely alarmed at some monopolies which infringed upon their financial status, and they attacked the increasing economic concentration of power on the stump and in the halls of the legislature, but they were inclined to believe that a few laws restricting corporations and protecting labor were all that was necessary along economic lines. There was no sign of a program to improve the economic condition of the underprivileged in the poorest of states."

Instead of disappearing after World War I, the Progressive impulse matured into a political and social philosophy emphasizing not only stabilizing reform and internal improvements but greater emphasis on economic development as a responsibility of the state. Underlying this responsibility was the assumption by the "Business Progressives" of the 1920s that most of their state's or community's problems could be solved by a healthy dose of economic growth. Thus these reformers, sounding the trumpet of progress at every opportunity, offered no challenge to traditional racial or class relationships, choosing instead to focus on the need for better roads, improvements in education and public health, and more efficient, "businesslike" government. A contemporary observer quoted by George B. Tindall provided this assessment: "The business class political philosophy of the New South is broad enough to include programs of highway improvement, educational expansion and health regulation. But it does not embrace any comprehensive challenge to laissez faire ideas in the sphere of relationship between capital and labor, and the section is lagging in social support of such matters as effective child labor regulation and compensation legislation."

"Progress" was not free, however, and especially by southern standards neither was it cheap. The rationale for increased expenditures for education rested on the returns gained from increasing the productive potential of the individual. Even tight-fisted representatives of the textile industry accepted the need for educational overhaul, arguing that "Expenditures Produce Prosperity" because "The man who is educated starts new enterprises or engages in new lines of business that pay taxes." In addition to increased expenditures for education, North Carolina spent so heavily that the state ended the decade eleventh in the nation in terms of surfaced road mileage.

Although the Business Progressive reform of the 1920s involved higher taxes and greater debt, southern tax rates remained comparatively low, and local option on valuation and collection helped to protect those with friends in the courthouse. Urban spokesmen endeavored to improve the quality of life in their cities only insofar as this could be achieved without raising taxes and public debt to levels that scared away business and industrial investors. Meanwhile, the county and small-town elites accepted the benefits of these new and expanded programs, secure in the knowledge that their influence over state and local politics would protect them from any serious challenge to their status or economic interests. Business Progressivism represented a marriage of reform and New South boosterism so enduring that, as Tindall observed, it "became by and large the norm of southern statecraft in the decades that followed."

Industrial promotion gained general acceptance as a legitimate goal of state government after World War I. Alabama, North Carolina, Florida, Virginia, and other states established commissions and agencies designed to publicize their advantages and contact prospective investors. Initially the development campaign focused primarily on the cities, where chambers of commerce and other booster organizations shouldered the responsibility for community economic progress. Policymaking in major southern cities came under the influence of commercial/civic elites ostensibly committed to orderly, controlled growth, but often given to wooing any and all industries with Grady-like abandon. The case of Louisville was typical. A post-World War I recession left the city with boarded-up businesses and a dwindling population. In 1917 a group of local boosters concluded that Louisville needed a "million-dollar factory fund" similar to ones used in other cities to subsidize industries and/or combat unions. The money was raised by high-pressure appeals to civic patriotism, as well as some zealous exaggeration of the financial returns from investments in the essentially nonprofit "Louisville Industrial Foundation." The Foundation used its funds to make loans to promising enterprises unable to obtain risk capital elsewhere. Some of these loans, such as the one to the then-struggling Reynolds Metal Company in 1918, paid off handsomely in later years.

The urban South's fervent pursuit of growth was best exemplified by the "Atlanta Spirit," an emotional dose of boosterism that inspired civic and business leaders to a new frenzy of smokestack chasing. The Atlanta Spirit was a lineal descendant of the New South ethos. Its spokesmen insisted that the region's economy could be transformed without destroying either regional charm or the racial and political traditions on which the vaunted conservatism and stability of southern society rested. Elsewhere in the urban South the emphasis was also on economic growth. "EXPANSION! EXPANSION! EXPANSION!" trumpeted the *Atlanta Constitution*, and in Memphis even the Ku Klux Klan joined in zealous local boosterism by making "A Bigger and Better Memphis" the theme of its 1923 political campaign. On the other side of the color line, a black writer in Norfolk concluded that "A city cannot thrive unless it has large payrolls . . . It cannot have large payrolls unless there are big factories, big railroad and shipping terminals and shops, big grain elevators and other industries."

The rabid urban boosterism of the 1920s led some southern writers such as Thomas Wolfe to raise serious questions about their region's obsession with the "Yankee way" and the ascendance of "cheap Board of Trade boosters, and blatant pamphleteers" to whom "progress" apparently consisted of "more Ford automobiles [and] more Rotary clubs." Another observer bemoaned the disappearance of a South "where man drew the fullness of his humanity from the land; where leisure, though not indolence, was the ideal; where people lived, not merely made a living."

The most straightforward and intelligent critique of the pursuit of industrialism came from the Nashville Agrarians, twelve conservative writers who contributed to *I'll Take My Stand*, a collection of essays published in 1930. The Agrarians took a stand to the effect that the South would be better served by efforts to preserve its traditional agrarian heritage than by attempts to subject it to the "tyranny of industrialism." In an emotional indictment of industrial society the Agrarians warned against subordinating human values to those of the marketplace and destroying the harmonious relationship between man and nature by uprooting southerners and placing them in an "unnatural" urban, industrial environment.

Although they were critical of industrialism, the Agrarians were not opposed to all industrial development. In fact, they favored limited industrial expansion as a means of providing balance in an agriculture-dominated economy. Unfortunately for the Nashville conservatives, their writings, though completed during the relative prosperity of the 1920s, appeared after the Depression had exposed the weakness of the South's economic base. Thus the Agrarian defense of tradition seemed also a defense of the poverty that had beset the South since the Civil War. Tradition was, after all, neither edible nor acceptable as legal tender. As Idus A. Newby noted, the contributors to *I'll Take My Stand* appeared to be "urging southerners to stay the growth of industry and cities at a time when most southerners saw such growth as the only way out of the South's economic problems."

The Agrarians appeared oblivious not only to their region's economic woes but to its social and political deficiencies as well. In celebrating a laudable version of the ideals of the "traditional" South, they also appeared to sanction a status quo characterized by racism, one-crop agriculture, illiteracy, tenancy, and a host of other problems. Critics such as Clarence Cason criticized the Nashville writers for taking "no account of contemporary social evils so often traceable in the opinion of other southerners to the very way of life the agrarians attempt to uphold." H. L. Mencken had little patience with the Agrarian "Habbakuks," whom he urged to stop spinning "lavender fancies under a fig tree" and turn their energies to solving the South's many problems. Mencken probably reflected the opinions of most liberal southerners and a great many of the region's political and civic leaders when he declared: "The mills and factories are there to stay, and they must be faced. Nothing can be done to help the farmers who still struggle on, beset by worn-out soils, archaic methods and insufficient capital. They are doomed to become proletarians and the sooner the change is effected the less painful it will be."

If critics were justified in upbraiding the Agrarians for their naivete in ignoring their region's deficiencies, then the South's industrial advocates were also deserving of rebuke for their equally naive contention that economic growth would automatically dissolve Dixie's social and institutional woes. This assumption was encouraged not only by the southern Babbits but indirectly and perhaps unwittingly by many prominent academics, particularly the Regionalists, a group of social scientists headquartered at the University of North Carolina. Led by Howard W. Odum, these researchers systematically studied problems and offered solutions, attributing southern backwardness to poverty, educational and cultural deficiencies, and blind sectionalism, and placing great faith in industrialization and urbanization as panaceas for these ills. By suggesting that economic expansion would automatically trigger social and political progress, the Regionalists set the tone for two generations of social scientists studying the process of change in the South, and reinforced rather than reassessed the all-out pursuit of industry that became a regional obsession in the 1930s.

Already an article of faith in the cities, the New South ethos conquered the countryside in the 1920s and 30s. Its widespread acceptance resulted both from rapid expansion of the urban South and from economic decline in the rural areas and small towns, especially in the Deep South, where worn-out soil and the invasion of the boll weevil combined to undermine the cotton production and processing that was the mainstay of the economy. The effects of the boll weevil on cotton yields may be gauged by looking at Greene County, Georgia, an especially hard-hit area where the total number of bales produced annually fell from 21,500 in 1919 to 326 in 1922. In 1924, as the boll weevil threatened to bring the state's economy to its knees, the Georgia legislature approved a measure allowing local tax exemptions for new industries.

Coming on the heels of the boll weevil invasion, the Depression further weakened the foundation of the cotton economy. The decline of the tenancy system, accelerated by the Depression, was further encouraged by some of the proposed remedies for agriculture's ills, particularly the Agricultural Adjustment Act. This acreage reduction plan also proved to be a sharecropper reduction measure, lessening the planter's need for labor by encouraging him to cultivate less land. During the first seven years that AAA policies were in effect, the thirteen cotton states saw their sharecropping population decline by nearly one-third as the number of agricultural workers fell to below one-third of the work force. Moreover, since the landlord theoretically had to share the AAA parity payment with his "croppers" he had an extra incentive to reduce them to wage-hand status whenever possible.

The New Deal's injection of cash into the southern cotton economy also accelerated the process of mechanization, allowing fewer farmers to cultivate more acres consolidated into a smaller number of farms. More machines naturally reduced the need for labor—either by cropper, tenant, or wage hand. Historian Pete Daniel noted the symbolism of the almost simultaneous disappearance of mules and sharecroppers. The suddenly superfluous agricultural worker faced the choice of out-migration or, if he could find it, employment in industry.

The industrial base of the Depression-racked South was too weak and narrow to take up much of the slack left by the constriction of the region's farm economy. Although the South had considerably more industry in 1930 than in 1865, the overall economic impact of industrial development in the region had been disappointing. The South's dependent relationship with the North continued in the twentieth century as the region provided raw materials and human resources and looked to other sections for capital, expertise, and manufactured goods.

Most of Georgia's factories were concentrated in such industries as textiles, turpentine, lumber, fertilizer, cotton seed oil, or railroad machine shops. Even these rudimentary enterprises were often financed by "foreign" capital. In 1880 only 12 percent of the state's nonagricultural wealth was owned by non-Georgians; forty years later this figure had risen to 28 percent.

By 1932 only 9 of 200 important southern corporations had their headquarters below the Mason-Dixon line. Names like Mellon, Goodyear, and Goodrich indicated that major national firms had begun to recognize the advantages of a southern location, but an already capital-scarce region's economic deficiencies were unlikely to be remedied by the expansion of companies whose profits went elsewhere. Writing in the 1930s, Howard W. Odum noted: "Although it now fabricates a considerable portion of its raw materials, its manufacturing processes are still largely confined to the more elementary levels. The South makes cast iron pipe, steel rails, girders, bolts, wire, steel plate and sheet, fabricates its skyscrapers, factories, its bridges, its oil and gas tanks, but imports its machinery, hardware, locomotives, and automobiles."

Although by 1910 most of the South's large cities contained a higher percentage of workers in manufacturing and mechanical jobs than in commercial pursuits, the urban South's economy remained largely commercial. On the eve of World War I, Atlanta's $340 million in trade dwarfed its $41 million in manufacturing. All of Georgia's railroads led to Atlanta, carrying the products of farm, forest, and factory into the capital to be dispersed to northern cities for processing and distribution. In the other direction, products from midwestern farms and northern factories were funneled through the city on their way to small-town shops and country stores.

Despite the rapid urban growth of the 1920s, at the end of the decade less than 25 percent of the South's income was derived from manufacturing. With its agriculture ailing and its industry underdeveloped, the South had little chance of fighting off the Great Depression. Per capita income in the region, 51 percent of the national average in 1880, rose to 62 percent by 1920 only to fall back to 55 percent by 1930. When a vexed Franklin Roosevelt described an impoverished, dispirited South as the "Nation's Number One Economic Problem," southern leaders disagreed vehemently, but Roosevelt's words rang true for large numbers of southerners who faced a daily struggle for survival.

The threat they faced was less immediate but the cumulative effects of boll weevil, drought, Depression, and relief programs plunged many members of the southern middle class into their own struggle for survival and weakened their ties to a shrinking plantation economy. Many merchants and professionals realized that demand for goods and services was certain to continue declining if outmigration could not be stemmed by providing alternative employment for labor no longer needed on the farm. The diminished labor requirements of the mechanized plantation also diminished the likelihood of planter-industrialist conflict over labor. With agriculture assuming a less dominant position in the region's economy, the quest for industrial development, which had already captured the imagination of the urban South, found new recruits in the small towns and county seats for whom a future of total dependence on agriculture was no longer viable.

Across the region, business and civic leaders in depressed towns and communities used public subscription drives to raise money to underwrite industrial development subsidies. Some enterprising boosters fashioned schemes whereby employees contributed to their own factory's "building fund" by allowing deductions from their pay checks. Such a method financed a factory in Dickson, Tennessee, where workers sacrificed 6 percent of paychecks that often totalled less than $10 per week. Albany, Georgia, leaders raised $10,000 to subsidize a new hosiery plant when executives promised to hire high school graduates who were to be paid only after successful completion of a six-month training period. Such questionable practices reflected the desperation with which southern communities approached the challenge of recruiting new industry. Similarly, the generosity of most communities sprang from the heated competition for the payrolls needed to revive flagging local economies and to stem out-migration.

No towns were more in need of economic stimulation than those in Mississippi, the South's and the nation's poorest state. The boll weevil had ravaged southwestern and northeastern counties, and economic contraction spelled the end of the line for many small-town merchants and professionals in these areas. The 1920s had witnessed the final destruction of the state's timber resources, and by 1930 even the fertile Delta counties were suffering. Columbia, in Marion County, was particularly hard hit. By the end of the 1920s local forests had been depleted by timber companies whose management had made no investment in reseeding. Hugh Lawson White had made his fortune by felling local trees, and the White Lumber Company had been the area's major employer. When White shut down his Columbia operations, a severe local recession underscored the need for new industry. Elected mayor at the end of the 1920s, White felt some responsibility for his role in the community's economic distress and he led a bold crusade to bring new industry into Columbia.

Several agricultural processing plants provided a few jobs, but White's major accomplishment came when he secured an agreement from the Reliance Manufacturing Company to construct a shirt-making plant in Columbia. In order to attract Reliance, White managed to raise $85,000 to construct a factory building which would become Reliance's property at the end of a ten-year period during which the company pledged to employ at least 300 workers (mostly female) and dispense a payroll of $1 million. Columbia quickly attracted two more factories and in 1931 Hugh White announced his candidacy for governor, promising that, if elected, he would "Balance Agriculture with Industry" in Mississippi. Defeated in 1931 but victorious in 1935, White secured legislative approval for his "BAWI" plan in 1936. The White Program authorized the use of municipal bonds to construct factories to house industries willing to commit themselves to a stipulated number of employees and/or a guaranteed payroll. The subsidized project was subject to the approval of a three-member Industrial Commission, then to majority vote in a local referendum.

The BAWI plan held several advantages for both industry and the subsidizing community. Municipal bonds were exempt from federal taxation and thus could be sold at lower interest rates than other securities. The result was an often substantial savings in finance costs. At the outset these costs were borne largely by the subsidizing community, which made the building available to the industry at a nominal rent. Under BAWI a company might lease a building for from $1 to $1,000 a year, write off the rental payments as operating expenses, and pay no property taxes because the building remained public property and thus tax-exempt. Some companies apparently purchased the securities which had been issued to construct their plants, thereby collecting tax-exempt interest payments on the bonds which were providing them with a low-cost building.

By the end of the 1930s the BAWI plan had subsidized twelve plants in Mississippi, including a hosiery mill at Grenada, a tire plant at Natchez, and a shipyard at Pascagoula. The state legislature allowed the program to expire in April 1940, but concern about heightened post-World War II competition for new industry rekindled support for BAWI, as did the fact that by 1944 all twelve subsidized plants were operating at full capacity, employing 14 percent of Mississippi's industrial work force. In response to public and political pressure the legislature quickly reenacted the BAWI plan and by the end of the 1950s firms established under both the first and the second bond subsidy programs employed 36,000 Mississippians and dispensed more than $100,000,000 in paychecks.

More significant than the program's contributions to Mississippi's economy was the spread of the BAWI idea across and out of the South. Tennessee, Alabama, and Kentucky quickly embraced the concept of bond-financed factories, and by 1962 nine southern and twelve nonsouthern states were in the bond subsidy business. Instead of the "full faith and credit" securities of the early BAWI variety, these new subsidy programs relied on revenue bonds which were backed not by the municipalities issuing them but by the subsidized industry's rental payments on the building financed by the bonds. Such bonds were still tax-exempt and thus offered finance cost savings to industrialists by transferring a municipality's borrowing advantages to private industry.

There were certain problems with the widespread use of municipal industrial securities. First, unsubsidized industries were left at a disadvantage because they had to pay higher financing costs. Second, as municipal issues grew larger, the federal government was losing considerable revenue. In 1966, had their interest been taxable, municipal bonds would have contributed well over $26,000,000 to the United States Treasury. Finally, the expansion of industrial issues made it harder to market more traditional "public purpose" municipal securities, such as those intended to finance schools, streets, or hospitals.

Bond subsidization drew criticism from financiers who viewed the practice as "socialistic" and "reckless." Labor union leaders assailed bonding programs because they encouraged the relocation of industry in areas where antiunion sentiments were deep-seated and institutionalized. The overall result was a loss of union influence. Industrialists prepared to move to nonunion locations were seldom afraid of strikes and thus had little incentive to engage in serious bargaining with their workers. The most vocal opponents of industrial development bonding were northern political spokesmen such as Senator John F. Kennedy of Massachusetts, who sought to close federal tax loopholes that could be used to lure industries away from their states or districts. By mid-1966 fourteen bills had been introduced to curtail the use of municipal bonds for industrial subsidy. For the most part these measures died at the hands of skillful, determined southern representatives whose seniority enabled them to obstruct legislation which they felt would be damaging to their state's efforts to attract new industry. Meanwhile, the aggregate value of industrial development issues skyrocketed. Approximately $1.39 billion in industrial securities appeared in 1967 alone. Many of these issues were for the benefit of major corporations whose executives appreciated the savings in financing costs afforded by bond subsidies. Although the South had no monopoly on the use of industrial bonds, by the end of the 1960s southern states still accounted for an overwhelming majority of such issues. The bonding frenzy came to an abrupt halt in 1969 when Congress followed the lead of the Treasury Department by removing tax exemptions from industrial issues larger than $5 million. This action reduced drastically the size of industrial bond issues until 1978, when Congress raised the exemption limit to $10 million, thereby facilitating another dramatic expansion of the use of bond subsidies.

In addition to bond financing, most state and local governments in Dixie were prepared to offer some sort of tax exemption to incoming industry. For example, in 1948 alone Louisiana governments forfeited in exemptions an amount roughly equal to 20 percent of that year's total tax collections. Between 1958 and 1961 Louisiana, Alabama, Mississippi, South Carolina, and Kentucky granted exemptions valued at an estimated $143,040,000. Industrialists minimized the effectiveness of tax exemptions as locational incentives, but Westinghouse Electric Corporation and other large firms gratefully accepted tax breaks on new facilities constructed in the South. Critics argued that exemptions denied state and local governments the new revenues that made industrial growth beneficial to the community. These revenues were often needed to provide the expanded services and facilities necessary to keep pace with industrial growth, especially if that growth resulted in a significant influx of new residents. Defenders of tax exemptions insisted that without them there would be no growth and that after the exemptions expired (normally a period of from five to ten years) the industrial property would begin to pay its own way as far as taxes were concerned.

Tax exemptions often went hand-in-hand with other official and quasi-official subsidies such as free or low-cost land and buildings or low- or no-interest loans provided by local development groups such as the Louisville Industrial Foundation. In 1941 the Dallas Chamber of Commerce purchased a 526-acre tract which became the site of a Convair bomber plant. Other communities constructed industrial parks which provided prime sites complete with convenient highway and rail connections and often with discounts on utility rates. In 1960 local business leaders in Bowling Green, Kentucky, formed an industrial foundation to acquire potential industrial sites. A fundraising drive netted $110,000 for the purchase of land for an industrial park, which was soon filled with blue-chip industries. Boosters were so pleased with the results of their efforts that they acquired more land and began recruiting industries for a second park.

Critics of subsidy programs often seemed to forget that most areas of the South had little to offer a new plant except an unskilled labor force and access to whatever raw materials might be nearby. Since most southern locations were equally attractive in this regard, local development activists were prepared to offer any and all giveaways and gimmicks likely to catch an industrialist's eye. Supporters of subsidy programs argued that political and economic leaders of depressed communities had to offer industrial subsidies in order to survive. Said one: "You listen to the experts tell you 'No!' Then if you are wise, you do whatever it takes!"

In many cases such enthusiasm for subsidies seemed to have been borne out. Basically, a subsidy amounted to an investment in a payroll. The addition of a new payroll to a local economy was presumed to induce a "multiplier" effect, wherein increased spending stimulated commerce and generated spinoff employment in such areas as services and construction. Many southern leaders were encouraged to subsidize by figures compiled by the Chamber of Commerce of the United States, projecting that 100 new industrial jobs might boost local income figures by $710,000, create 65 new nonindustrial jobs, and spawn 3 new retail establishments. When a Goodyear plant brought 1,400 new jobs to Lawton, Oklahoma, retail sales jumped by $8 million and bank deposits by $7 million. Would-be subsidizers argued that similar results in their own communities would soon make further subsidies unnecessary.

Assuming that subsidies were effective locational inducements, most development leaders at the state and local levels felt them a worthwhile risk when weighed against the prospective benefits they might produce. Seen in this light, subsidies made sense, although the use of giveaways and special concessions did not necessarily benefit every member of the community. Along with newly employed workers, local merchants and professionals were the major beneficiaries of public subsidies to industry, but the costs (in terms of increased taxes for bond interest or expanded services to new industries) were distributed throughout the population, many of whom did not benefit directly from the expansion of local industry. Public educators, for example, had little reason to celebrate the opening of a new plant that made little or no contribution to the local tax base or their salaries, and could at the same time lead indirectly to larger classes and a higher cost of living resulting from increases in housing prices and overall demand for consumer goods.

Ironically, although subsidies were designed to improve a state's or community's bargaining position by making it more attractive to new industry, such concessions actually left southern development leaders at a disadvantage. The ready availability of subsidies encouraged executives of footloose plants to make brazen demands on the communities wooing them. Augusta, Georgia, boosters offered a free building to a prospect, who responded with a counterproposal that included a lengthy list of alterations and repairs to the building. The industrialist also requested free water, power, highway, and railroad connections, as well as a five-year tax exemption. Finally, the company demanded that the city underwrite half the cost of training workers and contribute up to $5,000 to the firm's moving expenses.

In effect, a subsidy amounted to an investment in the new industry. Once a community had put its "full faith and credit" or at least its fiscal reputation on the line by issuing industrial development bonds to build a plant, that community had a stake in the future of that plant. Further demands on the part of the plant's executives, no matter how audacious, had to be met. When the General Shoe Corporation, which occupied an old building in Gallatin, Tennessee, received offers of a new building from five other towns, Gallatin residents quickly voted a $45,000 bond issue to keep the plant in their community. Star City, Arkansas, passed an ordinance requiring union organizers to pay a license fee of $1,000 per day because executives of the city's subsidized garment plant threatened to move elsewhere unless they were promised protection from unions. Promoters also often yielded to pressure from subsidized industries to refrain from recruiting new plants that might boost local wage scales.

With a subsidized employer in such a position of strength, the "company town" atmosphere was far more likely to develop. Kannapolis, North Carolina, population 37,000, retained the dubious distinction of being "the largest unincorporated town in the United States" in order to provide a tax-free haven for the area's dominant employer, Cannon Mills. Under the direction of Chairman of the Board Charles A. Cannon, Cannon Mills became the owner of most of the city's housing and the central business district as well. Cannon Mills also selected and paid the entire Kannapolis police force and used its control of the local water supply to keep out other industries that might bid up wages.

In the long run, the use of subsidies tightened rather than loosened the grip of traditional New South industries on the region's economy. This was true in part because subsidies were most appealing to industries such as textiles, apparel, footwear, hosiery, and furniture where intense competition made all costs, and therefore all savings, significant. For example, in 1951 a typical textile plant benefiting from the lower finance costs afforded by Mississippi's BAWI bonds could remain solvent at approximately 2 percent less profit than an identical nonsubsidized plant would have required. Most firms in competitive industries were also highly sensitive to labor costs and thus were already predisposed to seek a southern location. Subsidies were merely an extra incentive which helped to confirm a preexisting pattern. It was small wonder that by 1961, apparel, textile, food, and lumber and wood products operations still accounted for 52 percent of all BAWI industries.

New South development spokesmen had based their appeal to new industry on the region's "natural" advantages—an abundance of cheap labor and plentiful raw materials ready for processing. The desperation of the Depression years and the competitive intensity of the postwar period had encouraged development leaders to turn increasingly to certain man-made incentives intended to supplement their state's "natural" attraction for industry. Bond subsidies, tax concessions, and other gifts soon became the norm as the southern states tried to outbid their neighbors for new plants. Because, for the most part, every state offered the same advantages, such subsidies seemed to cancel each other out. Yet once these concessions were readily available almost anywhere in Dixie, no state's or community's leaders were willing to risk abandoning the practice of subsidization.

The increasing reliance on subsidies to attract industry to the South went hand-in-hand with intensified efforts to publicize the region's advantages and persuade investors to locate their new operations in Dixie. Many of the state and local organizations that were to play such a prominent role in promoting the twentieth-century South's industrial development were born in the post-World War I decade. In order to obtain New Deal dollars during the Depression the southern states joined a national move toward planned economic growth by establishing state planning commissions. Wartime prosperity and the prospect of intense postwar competition for new plants encouraged a shift in emphasis toward industrial recruitment, however, and most southern state planning and development agencies were largely committed to the latter responsibility by the end of the 1940s.

State development agencies sought out prospective investors likely to be interested in locating a new facility in one of the state's communities. By the end of World War II these agencies were relying on advertising, letters, phone calls, and personal visits by agency representatives to spread the good word. In their sales pitches state development staff members emphasized the traditional advantages of cheap labor, low taxes, and cooperative government. If an industrial prospect showed even an inkling of interest, state promoters were quick to follow up with offers of assistance, including a list of prospective sites which seemed to meet the manufacturer's general requirements. State developers were usually able to supply information about communities where free or low-cost buildings awaited new companies as well as information on tax exemptions and labor force estimates, which, of course, always reflected a more than ample supply of willing workers.

Keen competition among the southern states assured the prospect of kid-glove treatment by industrial development representatives. One manufacturer coyly responded to a North Carolina magazine ad: "Please pardon this letter, but I was reading *Time* magazine having just returned from a location in Kentucky and am waiting now to be picked up to go to Mississippi."

In the face of such intense competition, development leaders fretted about their state's image in the eyes of investors. Every plant work force that voted to organize was a threat to labor stability and every tax increase was another blemish on the state's all-important "business climate." A concerned director of South Carolina's State Development Board solicited the assistance of Governor George Bell Timmerman, Jr., in keeping the Palmetto state's income taxes low:

> The United States Rubber Company had a group that visited South Carolina, Georgia, Alabama, and perhaps other places. They were very profoundly impressed with South Carolina, particularly Greenwood. Since their return to New York, they have written us that the income tax of Georgia is much more favorable than that of South Carolina. . . .
>
> We have lost several plants to Georgia, and it is now apparent that the income tax story has probably been the cause.

By the mid-1960s, state industrial development efforts were so extensive that the budgets for such activities were usually at least $250,000 annually, and in several states these expenditures exceeded $1 million. These appropriations supported large suites of offices, experienced, professional staffs, and branch offices in large northern cities. Despite budgetary variations, industrial development had obviously become a major priority for every southern state.

Zeal for new industry quickly transformed southern governors into supersalesmen for their states. Before World War II most governors did little more to recruit new plants than write an occasional letter to an especially "hot" prospect. As competition became increasingly intense, however, governors not only wrote more letters but began making phone calls and even paying personal visits to potential investors. Luther Hodges of North Carolina implored a Ford Motor Company executive: "Please let us hear from you and we will be glad to fly out there to see you and your people anywhere you say." Hodges was also a pioneer in making industry-seeking trips to the North, a practice which became widespread in the 1960s. Gubernatorial "prospecting" tours consisted of luncheons and private meetings with industrialists, usually conducted at a breakneck pace.

It is difficult to determine the effectiveness of such personal salesmanship, but it clearly reminded voters back home that their governor was committed to his state's industrial growth. News that a southern governor had "bagged" an industry—that is, secured a pledge from company executives to locate a facility in his state— often seemed to be perceived as a sectional victory for the southern underdogs over the rich and powerful Yankees. Many southern editors and politicians delighted in baiting northern leaders who complained about such industrial "piracy."

Southern governors were not alone among state officials in their crusading for industrial development. State legislators were usually more than willing to enact or modify statutes in such a way as to enhance the state's industrial growth. Most state legislatures granted special tax exemptions for new industries with little or no debate. A classic example of legislative cooperativeness came in June 1956 when South Carolina's lawmakers met in special session to amend the state's alien ownership law so that Bowater Paper, an English concern, could locate a plant at Rock Hill.

Governors expected and received the cooperation of the entire bureaucracy in their industry-seeking efforts. South Carolina's Water Pollution Authority also did its part in the Bowater affair by exempting the company from the most stringent provisions of a new pollution control statute. Development officials seldom hesitated to commit state highway departments to providing highway connections for any incoming factory.

Influential private citizens also enlisted in the industry-seeking crusade. In 1969 three Mississippi bishops joined in the effort to persuade General Motors executives to locate a facility in Jackson. In Arkansas, Winthrop Rockefeller became part of the campaign for economic growth by agreeing to head the Arkansas Industrial Development Commission. Utilities such as Mississippi Power and Light and Georgia Power Company actively supported industrial recruitment efforts, as did a number of railroads and financial institutions, including the Citizens and Southern National Bank. Developers could usually count on the assistance of satisfied industrialists who had recently moved into the state. One Mississippi executive urged his Ford Motor Company counterparts to consider a Magnolia State location, citing the state's "low living costs, low taxes, and low cost natural gas and electric power," and "a supply of workers who quickly adapt themselves to factory work and truly appreciate a good job."

Once the public officials and employees and private citizens who comprised the state's development team had done their work, local boosters accepted the responsibility for persuading an industrialist that their town or county was the best possible location for his new plant. Normally mayors and Chamber of Commerce heads led the local crusade for new industry, with the support of merchants, professionals, and the local media. At the local level the sales pitch to new industry often focused on low-cost labor. A Fort Smith, Arkansas, Chamber of Commerce official assured an air-conditioning manufacturer: "There is plenty of darn good labor within commuting distance, now making the base minimum wage. These thousands of rural dwellers have little or no rent to pay and grow or raise most of the food they eat. They enjoy low living costs. There are no better workers anywhere. They will be with you and for you and listen to no leaders except your own."

By the mid-1960s, most southern communities boasted at least one industrial development organization which publicized the town's advantages, underwrote whatever subsidies it offered, and took responsibility for negotiating with the industrial prospect. The competence and resourcefulness of local promotional groups varied, but many were veritable goldmines of information capable of supplying mounds of data, including not only maps of potential sites but lists of existing industry, distances from major cities such as New York and Chicago, average temperatures and rainfall levels, names and addresses of local physicians, and even garbage pickup schedules.

When a prospect showed enough interest to visit, local boosters did their best to insure that the industrialist would hear nothing that would distress him. A typical development team included not only employers willing to paint a rosy picture of the local labor scene but local merchants, financiers, lawyers, and physicians well-equipped to provide positive responses to questions about the community's religious, cultural, and social climate. Some local developers occasionally went overboard in their efforts to be hospitable. One Arkansas mayor persisted in having his wife entertain industrial prospects with lengthy piano solos.

State development agencies often provided programs designed to help communities make the best possible impression when a prospect came calling. The Arkansas Industrial Development Commission sponsored a "Six-Point Preparedness Program" in the hope that a prospect's visit would not be marred by unanswered inquiries or gaps in his itinerary during which a community's deficiencies might be discovered.

Such preparations for selling one's community seemed necessary because of the intense inter- and intrastate rivalry for new plants. Support for industrial growth became a matter of local patriotism, and leaders warned that neighboring towns and counties would "get ahead" if all of the community's citizens did not support the development effort. Promotional organizations whipped up support for industrial bond issues, usually with the cooperation of the local media, who equated opposition or even skepticism about such moves with disloyalty to one's friends and neighbors and lack of concern about the community's future. Local civic organizations, usually dominated by the merchants and professionals who led the development effort, also played a prominent role in rallying community support for industrial recruitment.

Intra-community competition was intense, and local boosters were generally reluctant to admit that their rivals had outdone them in saying what an attractive prospect wanted to hear. Bidding through subsidies, concessions, and secret promises occasionally resulted in last-second changes in a company's plant location plans. For example, executives of the Chrysler Corporation had apparently already selected Morristown, Tennessee, for a new air-conditioner plant when they were accosted by a contingent of boosters from Bowling Green, Kentucky, who had borrowed a plane for a flight to Detroit to make one final effort to bring the plant to their area. The last-second heroics apparently paid off because Chrysler built the 600,000-square-foot plant near Bowling Green. Such competitive fervor occasionally got out of hand, as in cases where overzealous boosters even tried to stir up resistance to a new plant in competing communities in the hope that the facility might then be located in their towns instead.

Both state and local development groups believed "It Pays to Advertise," and they approached the distribution of information to industrialists with more enthusiasm than did their counterparts elsewhere. The major emphasis in such development advertising was on the savings afforded by a southern location, particularly in the area of labor costs. Not only was southern labor cheap, it was "native born," a description apparently intended to capitalize on a prevailing stereotype of immigrant workers as particularly susceptible to overtures of union organizers. Thus a typical South Carolina ad boasted of "99.79 percent native born" workers who recognized "the primary position of capital" and respected "competent management."

Most states lost no opportunity to publicize the various subsidies they offered or the abundance of raw materials available to incoming industry. Southern communities also attempted to capitalize on their relatively underdeveloped economies, emphasizing an abundance of choice industrial sites plus plenty of "room to grow."

Stressing the willingness of government to cooperate with incoming industry, southern development ads also featured messages from the state's governor. Personal assurances and official invitations to visit were standard fare, and especially development-conscious chief executives such as George Wallace even provided readers with their office phone numbers. Like the rest of the region's development effort, promotional ads aimed at convincing industrialists of a state's or a community's earnest desire for new plants. The message of most ads was that of hospitality to industry which would be manifested in the cooperative attitudes of workers, business and professional leaders, and state and local officials. Such cooperativeness held out the promise of privileged status for industrial employers, including freedom from worry about higher taxes, pressure for higher wages, or the onslaughts of labor organizers. All of these conditions contributed to what promoters called a "good business climate" that, coupled with the numerous subsidies available, made the South so attractive to industry.

If the South's obvious earnestness was a key to its success in attracting investments, its "heart on its sleeve" affection for industry did nothing to improve the quality of the region's growth. Executives of new plants realized that they could practically write their own tickets, and they generally did so, tailoring their pay scales to local levels and demanding that future industries agree to do the same.

The post-Depression decades saw the emergence of an energetic, generally well-organized effort to sell the South to new industry. Subsidies, enticing advertisements, and solicitous treatment of prospects were all a part of the Dixie promotional package. However effective such tactics may have been in winning the hearts of new investors, at the end of World War II the structure of the South's economy still exhibited many of the weaknesses that had stymied the efforts of late nineteenth-century development leaders. Interregional wage differentials persisted, reflecting both low levels of unionization and a regional industrial mix typified by Georgia, where as late as the early 1960s, 75 percent of the work force in more than half of the counties still worked in the low-wage textile, apparel, and lumber and wood industries.

The South's failure to escape the New South pattern of industrial expansion should not be blamed on its industrial development policies. These policies, after all, were only the manifestation of the heritage of agricultural dependence that still haunted the South as it entered the second half of the twentieth century. The region's economy continued to be dominated by slow-growth, low-wage industries because buying power did not increase fast enough to stimulate the agglomeration of the market-oriented firms needed to accelerate and sustain economic expansion. Investment capital was still hard to come by. Managerial and production skills were still underdeveloped, and a persistent surplus of underemployed labor continued to dictate an appeal to labor-intensive industries which, as in the past, would do little to improve the South's relative economic standing. Efforts to sell the South met with some success, but the type of industries that were buying were unlikely to provide any quick remedies for the deficiencies that undercut efforts to bring the region into the nation's economic mainstream.

3. The Sunbelt South

William N. Parker has observed that "To bring the South . . . into the nation after the Civil War required not only a national policy of the scope of the New Deal . . . but also the assistance of massive jolts from physical, technological and extraneous market and political events." His observation was no less correct for the Depression era, before New Deal farm programs reinforced the physical devastation caused by the boll weevil and facilitated the technological advances that paved the way for the mechanization and consolidation of southern agriculture. Although World War II did not immediately neutralize the South's economic heritage, it played a major role in culminating the trend toward agricultural modernization. It also supplied the "massive jolts" from "extraneous market and political events" needed to expedite the long and difficult move from the shadow of the plantation to the edge of the nation's economic mainstream.

World War II stimulated the South's economy as never before, and it set the stage for a series of "GI revolts," reform movements that heralded a gradual but ongoing process of political and institutional modernization. At the same time, however, the prewar labor and business climate remained intact. As a result, the post-World War II South provided a more economically viable, politically sophisticated atmosphere likely to appeal to more dynamic industries while it retained the operating and cost advantages that all manufacturing firms found attractive.

The war provided a massive injection of capital for the South's economy. More than $4 billion dollars (36 percent of the national total) went into southern military facilities. So many trainees poured into Dixie's various armed service centers that one frustrated trainee charged that the entire selective service system was part of a plot to line the pockets of southern merchants. One report concluded that $4.4 billion went into southern war plants, and private investment may have pushed this total nearer $5 billion. A reasonable estimate suggested that the war expanded the South's industrial capacity by 40 percent. Between 1940 and 1944 the South increased its share of federal payroll recipients from 19 to 27 percent, the latter figure being roughly equivalent to the region's share of the nation's population. As a percentage of total income, spending by all levels of government doubled during the war, and although government disbursements declined when peace returned, they never fell back to prewar levels.

Between 1929 and 1948 southern per capita income rose from 47 to 64 percent of the national average, with nearly half of this gain coming between 1940 and 1945. Per capita income in the region tripled during the 1940s as the percentage of the work force employed in agriculture fell from 35 to 22, while the percentage employed in manufacturing climbed from 15 to 18. The population of southern cities rose by 30 percent during the war, and the region's traditional pattern of rapid small-town growth gave way to faster expansion of larger cities. As migrants streamed into southern cities, large numbers also moved into northern metropolises. Approximately 2.2 million more people left the region than entered in the 1940s, with three-fourths of this net population loss being accounted for by blacks.

A plant location study conducted at the end of the 1940s attested to the expansive effect of World War II on southern markets. The automobile and automobile parts industries were important examples. Both General Motors and Ford saw Atlanta as a prime distribution center and chose it as a location for new assembly plants. General Electric put a sealed beam headlight plant in Lexington, Kentucky; Hicks Battery built a new facility in Biloxi. Estimating that the plant could supply 25 percent of the company's market, B. F. Goodrich put a tire factory in Miami, Oklahoma, while Firestone put a new plant in Memphis.

The war also accelerated mechanization of agriculture, as witnessed by a new International Harvester tractor plant at Louisville and a cotton picker assembly facility at Memphis, obviously situated to serve the cotton-rich Delta areas of Mississippi and Arkansas. Converted defense plants played a major role in postwar industrial growth. International Harvester's Louisville operation was housed in an old war plant, as was the Allis Chalmers plant at Gadsden, Alabama. At Nashville, Vultee converted its aircraft plant into a stove factory.

Most of the trends of the 1940s continued in the 1950s, so that the changes of the two decades between 1940 and 1960 seemed even more dramatic. In this period, for example, the South's population shifted from 65 percent rural to 58 percent urban. Black out-migration continued to the tune of more than 1.5 million, but during the 1950s the South experienced a net gain of 330,000 whites, the overall result being that between 1940 and 1960 the black percentage of the southern population fell from 24 to 21. By 1960 employment in agriculture accounted for only 10 percent of the regional total, while manufacturing employment rose to 21 percent. Per capita income stood at 76 percent of the national average.

As of 1960 all of the major statistical indicators of economic well-being still put the South well behind the rest of the nation, but the infusion of capital provided by the war, coupled with the mechanization and consolidation of agriculture that was already underway when the war began, had given the region's economic prospects an important boost. Increasing numbers of more affluent, skilled residents signalled the arrival of the long-awaited potential for the growth of rapid, technologically sophisticated industries as well as those drawn to expanding urban areas populated by enough consumers with money in their pockets to constitute truly attractive markets.

No state gave earlier promise of achieving the goal of economic parity with the rest of the nation than Florida, which had long emphasized climatic and lifestyle advantages in its efforts to attract tourists, residents, and new industries. Early in the post-World War II period, the state's industrialists found it easy to recruit executives, scientists, and engineers. In fact, there was evidence that many of these people had come to Florida confident that they could find suitable employment after they arrived. Hence it was not surprising that the aircraft industry found Florida locations attractive or that aerospace firms moved so swiftly and smoothly into the state.

At the height of the aerospace boom of the 1960s, Florida was absorbing 3,000 in-migrants a week, most of them with educational and income levels well above the southern average. Combined with the state's thriving tourist industry, its population boom proved an irresistible lure to market-oriented industries. In fact, Florida offered industry the best of both worlds—a fast-growing mass of relatively affluent consumers and the abundant cheap labor, low taxes, cooperative government, and publicly financed industrial support programs available in other southern states. Moreover, Florida projected a far more sophisticated, respectable image than any of its southern neighbors. Its population was diverse and less "southern" in cultural and behavioral preferences. Its politicians were pro-business and conservative but had not engaged in the rabid demagoguery that had been all too common in other southern states during the civil rights era. In short, although it offered all the traditional cost advantages for residents and industries that were available elsewhere in the South, its respectable political conservatism and relatively sophisticated population made Florida seem almost non-southern.

Obviously ocean beaches and warmer climates could not be installed throughout Dixie, but if the rest of the southern states could provide enough affluent consumers and attract faster-growing industries, then their economies might also reach the "takeoff" point and move into a cycle of self-reinforcing growth. In the 1960s more and more industries appeared to discover that many parts of the South could provide access both to Florida's markets and to those of other areas of the eastern United States as well. Although for many years the states of the Northeast, Mid-Atlantic, and North Central areas had been the cornerstone of industrial America, the old Manufacturing Belt was clearly in decay by the 1970s, while the warmer, less congested states of the Sunbelt were attracting the lion's share of new industrial investment. The Sunbelt included several states outside the South, but most of the examples used to document Sunbelt growth were southern ones. Florida was usually cited as the quasi-region's fastest growing state and Houston as its most rapidly expanding city.

The key to the Sunbelt South's economic ascendance was its population growth. For decades the South had been the nation's foremost source of migrants to other regions, as both well-educated and deprived youths left to pursue what appeared to be greater op-

portunities elsewhere. By the mid-1950s the region's population drain
had begun to slow and by the 1970s the flow had actually reversed
itself so that Dixie showed a net gain of nearly 3,000,000 residents
between 1970 and 1976. Florida, the nation's prime beneficiary of
in-migration, enjoyed an increase during this period of 1,630,000
residents, a figure larger than the combined growth of 21 northeastern
and north-central states. Ironically, many workers who as youths
had left Dixie when their parents moved to higher-paying jobs in
northern factories responded to "streets of gold" stories by returning south in the 1970s. As children they had been called "hillbillies"
by their new northern classmates. As middle-aged adults they became
"Yankees" to their new associates in the Sunbelt South.

An increasing number of southern in-migrants were black. After
1970 the South began to attract more blacks than it lost, thereby
reversing a century-old trend. Sympathetic journalists delighted in
pointing out that some of these blacks were "returnees" who had
moved north during leaner years. Moreover, many were attracted
not only by the region's economic opportunities (a number of them
earned lower incomes than they had received in the North) but by
the prospect of escaping the urban "rat race" for a more comfortable lifestyle in a familiar and now friendlier South.

Such accounts of reverse migration by blacks often overlooked
persistent racial difficulties in the South, but there was little doubt
that the northern industrial states were the source of much of the
South's in-migration. A study of workers covered by Social Security showed that during 1973 and 1974 nearly 91,000 more such
workers left the North and headed for the South than were moving
in the opposite direction. Florida was the big winner in the migration sweepstakes, accounting for more than 62 percent of the region's
net gains during the period. New York was the North's biggest loser,
followed by New Jersey and Pennsylvania. Only five (South Carolina, Mississippi, Louisiana, Arkansas, and Oklahoma) of thirteen
southern states lost population in the exchange with the North.

If the relationship between migration and the creation of new jobs
was any indication, comedian Brother Dave Gardner had been correct when he asserted that the only reason so many people lived in
the North was that they had jobs there. When the South was finally
able to provide jobs, it had little difficulty in attracting new residents.

As impressive as they seem, the quantitative significance of such figures was easily overstated. Without Florida, where 90 percent of population growth was due to in-migration, more than 65 percent of the South's population expansion would have been attributable to natural increase. The South's 1.5 percent higher birthrate was a major factor in its impressive showing in population statistics.

In-migration was nonetheless a crucial component of the Sunbelt phenomenon. Traditionally a significant number of the South's out-migrants had been intelligent and resourceful youths who took their talents to other regions where their abilities might find more suitable challenges and earn greater rewards. A 1951 survey reflected this tendency, indicating that more than 44 percent of southern-born business leaders were pursuing careers in the North. By the 1970s, however, nonsoutherners moving into Dixie were significantly younger and better educated than the average American, and a 1977 survey showed that less than 21 percent of southern-born executives were pursuing their careers in the North. The influx of young managers and professionals was a shot in the arm to a middle class whose traditional anemia had contributed to the region's slow rate of overall growth. Dixie was rapidly developing the consuming class necessary for faster, self-sustaining economic expansion.

At the other end of the age scale, many of those who moved south were retirees. While the elderly population increase nationwide between 1970 and 1976 was approximately 15 percent, in the South this figure exceeded 22 percent. Lower living costs were understandably attractive to those on fixed incomes. A 1976 estimate put expenses in Boston at 36 percent higher than those in Austin. A warmer climate meant a simpler, relaxed lifestyle without snowshovels or winter driving hassles. Many retirees moved to the South at the behest of friends and neighbors who were pleased with the results of their own moves. Others uprooted themselves to be near children and grandchildren who had moved in pursuit of career opportunities. Military retirees, many of whom had spent a number of years stationed in the South, found it convenient to remain near their former homes in order to take advantage of medical and post exchange facilities. Between 1965 and 1970 the Northeast lost over 96,000 residents to armed services migration while the South was gaining nearly 108,000. Whatever their reasons for settling in the South, relatively few in-migrants seemed to regret their decisions. In the

1970s polls showed that nationwide only residents of the Mountain and Pacific states were more satisfied than southerners with the areas where they lived. Another poll of thirteen states that included North Carolina, Texas, Alabama, Louisiana, and Florida showed that resident satisfaction was higher in the five southern states than in any others studied except California, which ranked fourth.

Almost all indicators of economic growth showed dramatic progress in the Sunbelt South. For example, gross regional product nearly doubled between 1960 and 1975, while industrial output more than doubled. Between 1970 and 1976 fast-growing Texas added more nonfarm jobs than Michigan, Illinois, Ohio, and Massachusetts combined. In 1976 the industrial output of Texas alone exceeded that of Australia. Between 1970 and 1977 per capita income increased at a national average of 71 percent, while Arkansans and Mississippians saw their personal incomes rise by 86 and 83 percent, respectively. These states had traditionally been the South's slowest growing, and any significant increase would appear dramatic when considered on a percentage basis. Still, even in more economically advanced Florida, per capita incomes grew by 69 percent during this period as compared to only 58 percent improvement in New York.

Much of the South's growth was attributable to natural resources and energy reserves. By the 1970s the region accounted for well over one-third of the nation's commercial timberland and an equal proportion of its electric generating capacity. In addition, southern wells produced 65 percent of the nation's crude petroleum.

Energy demand was the key to explosive growth in Houston, where ninety-nine large industrial firms opened new operations between 1971 and 1978, bringing with them literally thousands of subsidiary operations. The city gave birth to 79,000 jobs in 1979 alone as unemployment fell below 3 percent and 1,000 new residents flocked in each week. Because Texas had neither a personal nor a corporate income tax, new Houstonians rejoiced at a per capita annual tax load of $175, $666 lighter than that of New Yorkers.

Many of the Sunbelt South's new industries were a far cry from the garment and textile sweatshops of the past. In 1977, for example, Sperry Rand opened a $6 million electronics component plant near St. Petersburg. Huntsville, Alabama, boosters built on the area's extensive defense payroll to attract a subsidiary plant of General

Telephone and other plants that were less labor intensive than most southern operations. Tennessee attracted several major new plants in 1980. The largest was a $3 million Datsun truck assembly facility to be constructed in Smyrna. Dickson, a town of 8,000, landed a $70 million *Parade Magazine* printing plant that would provide 400 new jobs and a $4.5 million annual payroll. Many large companies not only built new operations in the South but moved their home offices to Dixie as well. This was the case with Northern Telecom, Ltd., which transferred its American headquarters from Waltham, Massachusetts, to Nashville.

Most of the region's growth prior to 1970 came in manufacturing, but in the 1970s services such as banking, retail trade, and real estate expanded so rapidly that they soon accounted for well over half of the regional product. There was some debate as to whether the South was as seriously hit by the 1974-75 recession as the rest of the nation. Industries such as manufacturing and construction bore the brunt of the decline nationwide, but the growing service component of the South's economy promised to make it less susceptible to future economic downturns.

One of the most striking statistics concerning the Sunbelt South's growth was the fact that by the 1970s the region was attracting approximately half of the nation's total annual foreign industrial investments. The first significantly successful efforts to lure foreign industry to the South were those of North Carolina Governor Luther Hodges, who in 1959 had led a group of industry-seeking Tarheels on a two-week tour of England, the Netherlands, Germany, Switzerland, France, and Belgium. Hodges's efforts were soon emulated as other governors began traveling abroad as well as northward to seek new plants. By the 1970s European and Japanese industrialists were almost as likely to be contacted by southern development agencies as were their counterparts in the United States. Many major world cities had branch offices of state development agencies. Georgia, for example, established such outposts in Brussels, Tokyo, Sao Paulo, and Toronto.

Among the southern states the two Carolinas proved to be most successful at attracting foreign plants, and South Carolina's international recruitment program was usually cited as the region's most effective. By the end of the 1970s the Palmetto State was drawing 40 percent of its annual industrial investments from foreign sources.

South Carolina boosters could boast, for example, that there was more West German industrial capital in their state than anywhere else in the world except West Germany. The South Carolina community most affected by an influx of foreign plants was Spartanburg, which prior to the early 1960s had been dominated by an ailing textile industry whose dreary mills paid poorly and shut down often. The arrival of several foreign firms, particularly Hoechst Fibers in 1965, quickly launched a snowballing trend toward diversification. By the mid-1970s, 4,000 local workers were employed in foreign-owned plants, local income levels had risen dramatically, and unemployment had plunged.

There were several basic incentives for foreign industries to invest in the United States. First, there was the promise of long-term political stability and little fear of nationalization or government harassment. Second, an American location removed concerns about import quotas or tariff barriers. Finally, the decline in the value of the dollar made the investment in industrial property in the United States a particularly attractive one.

European investors chose southern locations because they still offered most of the South's traditional advantages for industry. Labor was still cheap, raw materials remained readily available, and state and local governments maintained their cheerful, cooperative attitudes. The Daiwa Spinning Company of Osaka, Japan, for example, chose Levelland, Texas, as a site for a $20 million plant after competitive bidding among 32 Texas towns resulted in Levelland's offer of land and accompanying rights for the sum of $10.00.

The South's mild weather was a decided plus, and for some foreign executives its nonunion labor climate was also appealing. A German industrialist who located in Mississippi indicated that his choice of a plant site was prompted by the same factors that brought many American firms to the region: "We hoped and we still hope that it will take a certain time until the unions move slowly down from the North to the South, and the farther down you are the longer it may take." He also linked the rise of the Sunbelt South to the demise of the Industrial North: "A lot of industry wants out of the North because of the high labor problems, because of people living together crowded in big cities—aggressive people giving problems to factories."

With only 2 percent of the local work force organized, the South

Carolina Piedmont was a near-perfect location for the union-fearing Michelin Tire Corporation. By the end of the 1970s the French company had responded to the cooperation of local officials and the favorable labor situation by employing over 5,500 workers at its South Carolina facilities. Firms from heavily industrialized nations such as Japan also favored a location in the southern United States because of the availability of space and the impression that heavy and potentially polluting industries such as textiles were still welcome.

The stimulus of increased industrial investment was reinforced by an ongoing pattern of significant federal spending in the South, where affection for the military remained strong even in the turbulent 1960s. Aggressive congressmen such as Mendel Rivers of South Carolina managed to cram their districts with military installations. Southern representatives were able to influence the flow of military money by maintaining a firm grip on the Armed Services and Appropriations committees of both the House and the Senate. By the 1970s the defense industry was the largest single employer in a number of southern states. In Huntsville, Alabama, construction of the Marshall Space Flight Center had helped to draw in such desirable private firms as International Business Machines and Rockwell International, but at times space and defense activities accounted for as much as 70 percent of Huntsville's total employment. Fort Sill's payroll and the 6,000 jobs it provided kept Lawton, Oklahoma, afloat until the 1970s when a new Goodyear plant pumped $20 million into the local economy. By the early 1970s southern states held nine of the top twenty-one spots in a ranking of "defense dependency" based on the percentage of total employment directly or indirectly attributable to defense spending. Non-defense-related federal programs such as the Area Redevelopment Administration, whose loans helped to finance many small plants, were also a boon to industrial development efforts.

The Tennessee Valley Authority provided both a large injection of capital and a number of services and improvements that facilitated industrial development. Low-cost electricity not only lit the homes of thousands of valley residents but powered scores of industries including such major defense facilities as the Oak Ridge Atomic Laboratory in Tennessee and the Redstone Arsenal in Huntsville.

By the early 1970s TVA produced about 10 percent of the nation's electricity. The Tennessee River bustled with barge traffic and its banks were lined with plants producing everything from chemicals and fertilizer to synthetic fibers and cement. TVA experts not only consulted with local farmers and timbermen about cultivation and resource management techniques, but provided advice and assistance to state and local industrial development organizations. Location surveys showed that labor costs and availability remained a major attraction for industries moving into the valley, but many of these firms also sought low-cost power. TVA was a major asset to the East South Central states in their efforts to promote economic growth.

In the 1970s some distressed representatives of the declining Industrial North insisted that the Sunbelt South's ascendance came at their region's expense. They charged that defense and federal aid spending policies which favored Dixie had actually subsidized the Sunbelt boom. In the mid-1970s some well-publicized reports supported their claims, revealing that in 1975 alone the southern states received $11.5 billion more in federal funds than they sent back to Washington in the form of taxes, while the ten northern states suffered a net deficit in this area of $30.8 billion. In that same year the South received approximately $212 more per resident in federal funds than did the Midwest.

The Sunbelt South also benefited greatly from changes in traditional interregional migration patterns. As the population of major metropolitan centers like New York City fell by 2,000 people per week and smaller cities suffered proportionately high losses, the industrial North was experiencing a drain of talented, tax-paying residents. Meanwhile, as leaders of northern cities sought to cope with shrinking tax bases and the intensifying problems of already disadvantaged central city populations, impoverished and unskilled southern out-migrants continued to arrive in these areas. From a tax base/human resource perspective, the South was getting the best of the bargain while northern state and local governments were continually forced to ask more of a population already burdened by heavy tax loads.

Had the South's political and economic leaders supplemented the impact of federal spending with some aggressive acts of "industrial piracy"? Many northern leaders complained that this was the case, citing well-publicized industry-seeking forays into the North by southern governors as well as the establishment of southern state development offices in many northern cities. Defenders of these efforts scoffed at northern charges, noting that less than 2 percent of job losses in the North resulted from the movement of factories out of the region. In fact, most of the North's industrial decline was due to the contraction or closing of firms at a time when new jobs were being created at a significantly slower rate in the North than in the South. Still, while it was technically correct that relatively few of the South's new plants had been "stolen" from Manufacturing Belt states, when industrialists considered the advantages of operating a plant in the South, they were more likely to close less profitable facilities in the North and construct new ones in southern locations.

For many years southerners had made little effort to conceal their glee when a northern investor yielded to the persuasive talents of a southern governor or industrial development representative and announced that he was building a new branch plant in Dixie. News of such decisions was so joyously received as to foster the suspicion that many southerners saw such "raids" on northern industry as a means of gaining revenge for their region's defeat in the Civil War. Northern cries of "plant piracy" first bore fruit in the 1968 congressional restrictions on the use of industrial subsidy bonds. The rapid growth of the Sunbelt South in the 1970s coupled with the obvious decay of the old Manufacturing Belt intensified calls for measures to prevent southern representatives from "stealing" industry from the North.

The increased determination of northern leaders to recoup their region's economic losses was reflected in a general equalization of state industrial development budgets nationwide and a vigorous effort to reduce the southward flow of federal funds. Shocked southern leaders called for collective action of their own as a "defensive" measure, and the Southern Growth Policies Board shifted its emphasis from regional planning to defense of regional interests. The "Sunbelt-Snowbelt" clash was compelling evidence that the 1980s might witness a new War Between the States, this one over jobs and payrolls.

There was considerably more to the Sunbelt story than federal favoritism and plant thievery. A combination of several theories of regional growth helps to provide some historical perspective. A general explanation for the relatively slow pace of growth before 1945 was the theory that during the late nineteenth and much of the twentieth century the South and the Industrial North were linked in a relationship that helped to insure unequal patterns of growth.

On the one hand, for much of the postbellum period deficiencies in market, capital, and labor quality made the South unattractive to most investors and potential in-migrants, and thus retarded the overall rate of southern industrial expansion. The thriving Manufacturing Belt's attractiveness to investors, entrepreneurs, and productive citizens forced the southern states to content themselves with the leftovers from the feast of northern economic progress. Still, there were some "trickle-down" benefits for the lagging, economically dependent South, as near obsolete, relatively inefficient industries that were unable to compete for capital and labor in the advanced industrial society of the Manufacturing Belt found new life in the form of lower production costs below the Mason-Dixon line. Thus, despite its disadvantages, the South still experienced slow but steady growth. Critics traditionally blamed this slow growth on policies that maintained the South as a colony operated for the benefit of northern industrial and financial interests. Economist Joe Persky probably came closer to the truth when he described the South as a "most favored" colony that had grown faster than most such areas because it had attracted investments in the older, competitive, labor-intensive industries that had developed in the neighboring regions of the same nation.

Ironically, there were even some benefits in the South's image of regional backwardness because rehabilitation of the South became a major national mission, especially after President Franklin D. Roosevelt proclaimed the region "The Nation's Number One Economic Problem." Agencies such as the Tennessee Valley Authority, the Area Redevelopment Administration, and the Appalachian Regional Commission made important contributions to economic development in the South.

The "trickle-down" benefits, coupled with the metamorphosis of the plantation system (itself accelerated by the impact of New Deal programs) helped to stimulate more rapid expansion, but the major factor in the South's economic "takeoff" was World War II, which provided the South with both investment and human capital that had previously been lacking. The impetus for rapid economic growth in the post-World War II South also derived from the demise of the Industrial North. The fate of the old Manufacturing Belt suggested that Joseph Schumpeter's theories concerning the ultimately self-destructive tendencies of capitalism were not without merit. The northern industrial belt was beset by many of the problems cited by Schumpeter, including declining investment opportunity and hostility to capitalism and entrepreneurs. Meanwhile, the Sunbelt South retained the advantages of a most-favored colony by offering a fertile area for investment and risk-taking, featuring a favorable business climate free from the higher taxes, social welfare demands, and labor aggressiveness that confronted industrialists in the North. Thus, ironically, the pattern of deferred growth that had frustrated southern leaders for so long finally helped to put the South in the right place at the right time. The post-World War II South, with its belatedly emerging markets and investment opportunities, presented investors and in-migrants with a positive and timely contrast to the North, whose once vibrant industrial economy had grown past maturity toward the brink of obsolescence.

It was difficult to determine which of the Sunbelt South's specific attractions were the most important in terms of luring industry. Cheap labor remained a major factor throughout the post-World War II period, particularly among competitive, labor-intensive industries where wages represented a sizable percentage of total operating expenditures. Textile executives, for example, consistently put the greatest emphasis in their site selection decisions on wage rates, or the local "labor climate" (often translatable as "How many unions are there in the community or close by?"). Textile, garment, and similar industries also paid attention to such factors as right-to-work and antipicketing laws, as well as the apparent willingness of local officials to provide employers with protection from unions.

Low taxes were important to incoming industries involved in competition significant enough to make all expenses count, although tax costs were seldom the primary factors in bringing industry into any state or community. Studies indicated that tax rates rarely influenced an industrialist's decision unless two or more sites were equally suitable for his new plant.

Raw materials were a key to attracting such industries as paper, petroleum, or clay. The pine belt of Georgia landed its share of pulp and paper plants, for example, while Louisiana and Texas were desirable locations for petroleum firms. The importance of raw materials as a locational consideration depended on the cost and convenience of transporting those materials.

What of markets? To what extent did they help to explain the Sunbelt South's dramatic growth? In the early postwar years optimistic observers probably overstated the attractiveness of the region's markets, but the growth of population and commercial centers like Atlanta soon triggered an agglomerative tendency among industries such as automobile manufacturing. Atlanta's automobile assembly plants helped to attract related operations to the city's hinterland, as in the case of United States Rubber at Opelika, Alabama, or Monroe Auto Equipment at Hartwell, in northeast Georgia.

The single greatest attraction the post-World War II South could offer market-sensitive industries was Florida's burgeoning consumer pool. Improvements in transportation meant that many southern locations would allow a firm to tap into the Florida market without sacrificing its connections elsewhere. Population expansion was a key to market attraction, contributing heavily to the growth of service industries such as restaurants, hotels, and wholesale distributors. Though labor-oriented firms remained a major source of jobs in the Sunbelt South, growth in market-related industries was nonetheless a crucial factor in the region's economic takeoff in the late 1960s and 1970s.

It is worth noting that the relative importance of these factors varied over time and among industries. Labor remained a crucial consideration even in the 1970s, but markets became increasingly important throughout the period, particularly after the Sunbelt boom began. For many years industries with relatively few worries about competition had little reason to fret about interregional differences in production costs, which they merely passed on to consumers. As southern markets grew and foreign competition became more intense, however, industries such as automobile manufacturing began to respond to the pressures to cut costs by taking advantage of the labor, tax, and finance savings a southern location could provide. The promise of savings in all these areas combined with the growth of Dixie's consumer markets to attract many industries that had traditionally shunned southern locations.

When the various factors that contributed to the growth of southern industry in the last two decades are considered separately, it is difficult to determine which was most influential. In the long run it may be safest to observe that not one but all of these factors, viewed in conjunction with the region's positive attitude toward business and industry, were the key to understanding the Sunbelt success story. A 1980 survey produced a state-by-state ranking of business climates that placed six southern states in the top ten ranks and gave the region an overall rank of 11.5 as compared to a northeastern average of 35.8 and a midwestern figure of 25.6. These rankings took into account factors such as tax rates, unemployment compensation levels, and labor relations histories.

The results of this survey, which appear to be closely related to the distribution of growth in manufacturing employment, indicate that basic economic considerations remained paramount as new plant sites were being chosen. Individual rankings by factor showed that eight of the nine states with the lowest tax load per capita and five of the seven with the lowest state spending levels per capita were in the South. Moreover, six of the seven states with lowest union membership were also in Dixie, as, not surprisingly, were five of the six with the lowest weekly manufacturing wage.

External pressure for institutional, political, and social progress also contributed to the South's economic advancement by spurring reforms that made Dixie a more respectable living environment for the relatively affluent in-migrants who helped to enhance the allure of the region's markets. Changes in the attitudes of Americans at large also enhanced the South's ability to attract higher-income, better-educated new residents. In a decade of resurgent conservatism and lowered expectations many Americans were willing to let bygones be bygones as far as the South was concerned, probably because recent national disappointments suggested that the problems still plaguing the South were also observable in the nation at large. Economic advancement and limited social and institutional reform had helped to "Americanize" Dixie, while post-civil rights, post-Vietnam, post-Watergate disillusionment had contributed to the "southernization" of the nation at large.

The importance of external factors should not obscure the fact that the South did much to aid its own cause. Industrialists consistently listed programs such as start-up training and state-supported research assistance among the key factors which influenced them to build plants in the South. In the long run, however, the ability to make the limited changes necessary to enhance its appeal to consumers and industries without abandoning key elements of the New South approach to industrial development accounted for much of the Sunbelt South's success. Continuing cost advantages in all areas, conservative government, and a cooperative, deferential attitude toward industry had been parts of the South's appeal since the Henry Grady era. Combined with new programs like research and training assistance, and a generally improved national perception of the region, traditional development policies helped to make the Sunbelt South appealing to almost all kinds of industries.

Glossy and modern as its showcase areas appeared, the Sunbelt South was actually a curious blend of the old and the new. Decades of slow growth had prepared the South for the rapid expansion of the 1960s and 1970s by preserving lower living and operating costs and an as yet unspoiled living environment. Ever a study in paradox, the South found that its heritage of underdevelopment had suddenly become beneficial without ceasing to be burdensome. Sunbelt growth was spotty, wages were still well below the national average, and a large number of southerners continued to live near or below the poverty line. The racial, political, and institutional climate was improving but considerable room for improvement remained. In short, the southern economy was prospering but not yet prosperous; southern society was progressing but not yet progressive. While some were tempted to proclaim at last the realization of a truly New South, others shared the skepticism of Charles P. Roland, who saw the South as "America's will-o-the-wisp Eden," a region whose destiny was to be "a land becoming and not a land become."

4. Life and Labor in the Industrializing South

Like the New South of the 1880s, the Sunbelt South of the 1980s continued to depend on cheap, relatively docile labor as its primary attraction to new industry. Critics correctly cited persistent interregional wage differentials as evidence of a century of labor exploitation, but for several generations of southern industrial workers it was also a century of slow but significant economic advancement.

For most southerners who became industrial workers in the late nineteenth century, the move into the factory amounted to swapping the incessant poverty of sharecropping or red-dirt small farming for the dreary, often disappointing existence afforded by the region's emerging labor-intensive industry. Hours were long, tasks arduous, and wages short in the New South's lumber and textile operations, but few who had the opportunity to return to the farm ever did so permanently. Flawed and exploitive as the blueprint for industrial expansion may have been, it represented for many deprived southerners their only apparent chance for a better life. As such, it was an offer that most of them simply could not refuse.

Cheap labor was the New South's primary attraction for new industry, and the story of the region's industrialization naturally involved considerable labor exploitation. There was no more damning evidence of the indifference to human suffering and exploitation on the part of many of the South's industrialists and public officials than the convict lease system. By leasing convicted criminals to lumber, mining, railroad, and other interests, as well as to plantation owners, southern state and local officials found a way to make crime pay. Instead of shouldering the burden of a growing prison population in a time of budgetary retrenchment they simply took advantage of the cheap-labor orientation of New South industry. In 1876, for example, a Georgia law allowed the leasing of the state's convicts to three "penitentiary" companies for a twenty-year period for the sum of $500,000.

The growth of the convict-lease system paralleled the expansion of laws that produced more convicts. Such a statute was the infamous Mississippi "pig law," which defined the theft of any livestock (or property valued at $10.00 or more) as grand larceny punishable by up to five years' imprisonment. With additional convictions meaning extra revenue for the state and often larger bribes for state penal officials, jurists faced pressure for speedy convictions and lengthy sentences. Rapidly losing any legal protection, blacks suffered most under the system. In 1878, for example, 1,124 of Georgia's 1,239 convicts were black. Perhaps the worst aspect of the system was the misery it inflicted on young people. In 1874 Tennessee leased 123 convicts under the age of 18. Five years later Georgia leased 132 boys between the ages of 11 and 17.

Despite legal language ostensibly guaranteeing the health and safety of the convicts, living and working conditions were wretched. One critic charged that the system made southern penal institutions "veritable nurseries of crime, anarchism and degradation." A report on conditions in the Mississippi penitentiary hospital described inmates marked by signs "of the most inhuman and brutal treatments. Most of them have their backs cut in great wales, scars and blisters, some with the skin peeling off in pieces as the result of severe beatings." Lying on the bare boards, the enervated prisoners were too weak to combat the "live vermin crawling over their faces." Under such conditions it was understandable that the annual death rate for convicts ran as high as 25 percent in some states. By 1919 only Alabama retained the convict lease system, but the exploitation of labor in southern industry was far from over.

No industry had a worse reputation for peonage and mistreatment of labor than did the southern timber and turpentine companies. As late as the 1930s, for example, Florida's Osceola Log Company recruited employees with promises of $4.00 per day in wages, neglecting to tell them that room and board would be deducted from that sum, as would purchases at a company commissary at drastically inflated prices. The company kept the books, and net wages could amount to takes like eight cents—for two weeks' work. Laborers whose purchases exceeded their wages had no choice but to remain until they "worked off" their debts. The gates of the workers' camps were locked at night and on Sunday, and the foremen doubled as weapons-toting guards.

Southern timber camps provided some striking examples of wage slavery and worker abuse, but the textile industry has received more attention from scholars seeking to understand southern labor's response to industrialism. The folk who became the first residents of these mill villages were recent migrants from the upland South's small farms and sharecropping plots. Bound by a common past, they were nonetheless in an unfamiliar environment and largely dependent on their employers not only for income but for housing, sustenance, and guidance.

Thus to some extent the mills and mill villages provided a context within which upper-class whites could practice paternalism toward their lesser white brethren. This brand of paternalism was similar to that of the sharecropping plantation, albeit somewhat more structured. The company store supplanted the supply merchant or the plantation commissary, and the pay might be in scrip redeemable only at the company store. Employers often supplied housing at little or no rent, although rental rates did not have to be excessive to represent a sizable portion of a family's take-home pay. In many unincorporated mill towns the company subsidized the churches as well as the schools. Thus it was not surprising that ministers preached obedience and loyalty, and teachers reminded pupils of their indebtedness to their parents' employer for their education.

Although many children who attended mill schools may have received a better education than they would have otherwise, educational expenditures were hardly a burden to the company. One South Carolina mill studied by David Carlton spent only one-third of 1 percent of its capital investment on schools. In 1900 Pacolet Mill school employed but four teachers to instruct 400 pupils. Overall, none of the mills Carlton studied spent as much as 1 percent of their total capital a year on projects relating to "social welfare."

Within the mill and the mill village there were often close ties between laborer and foreman, and working relations were typically relaxed and informal. Wilbur J. Cash may have overstated the case for the mitigating influence of piety and noblesse oblige on the mill owners' attitudes toward their workers, but he was probably correct in asserting that, all things being equal, most owners were not without concern for the health and welfare of their employees. In an age of laissez faire, however, most employers in the South and elsewhere refused to accept much responsibility for their labor force's working or living conditions. Cotton mills were seldom properly ventilated and were humidified in order to protect brittle threads. Workers had no choice but to breathe the lint-filled air that hung in the damp sweat box that was their workplace or to share drinking water from an open bucket equipped with a single dipper or gourd. Understandably, mill workers suffered from various lung disorders, often commonly diagnosed under the labels of "consumption" and "tuberculosis."

The configuration of housing in the early mill village was more reminiscent of the slave quarters than of the dispersed shacks of sharecroppers. Often lacking even doorsteps, the crudest mill village cabins were poorly built and as forlorn in appearance as their inhabitants. Substantial improvements in mill housing awaited World War I, when higher profits and dwindling labor supplies spurred remodeling and the installation of a host of such modern conveniences as plumbing, sewers, and electric lights.

Overcrowded housing and the density of the mill village would have allowed little enough privacy even without the snooping practiced by some mill officials. For example, the Roseville (North Carolina) Cotton Mills housed their superintendent and overseers in the first houses leading into the village so that they could oversee employee behavior and report on offenses such as women wearing shorts, smoking on their porches, or getting pregnant out of wedlock. Drunkenness was also difficult to conceal. One worker insisted: "You don't have no private life at all. . . . I used to pull a high lonesome once in a while, and I go back in Monday morning; first thing boss would say: 'You drunk Friday, Saturday, and Sunday.'"

In the late nineteenth century few of even the most paternalistic mill owners would have won praise for their generosity with their payrolls. There was considerable variation in the wage scales of southern cotton mills, but adult males who received $2.53 a week in 1885 were getting even less ten years later. Many mills employed more women than men, largely because they could handle most of the same jobs at a wage rate often only half that paid males. In certain Alabama industries between 1885 and 1895 male employment increased by 31 percent while female employment rose by 75 percent. Interregional wage differentials were striking. In 1900, spinners in New England mills earned 20 cents an hour, hardly an impressive wage unless it was compared with the 5 cents an hour earned by southern spinners in the same year.

Not only were wages low, but weeks were long, often as much as or even more than seventy hours (twelve to fourteen hours longer than New England work weeks). The practice of hiring whole families meant that young children were taken into the mills, often standing on boxes to tend machines they could not reach otherwise. In 1900, 30 percent of the South's textile force was under sixteen years of age. In the same year, 75 percent of the spinners in North Carolina mills were under fourteen. During heavy work periods when the mills operated on a pre-dawn to post-sunset schedule, parents occasionally carried their still-sleeping children to work in the morning only to bear the same exhausted offspring home in the evening. One labor leader claimed in 1887 that a Huntsville, Alabama, mill employed children as young as six, paying them only eight cents per day: "Women and children in the cotton factories are indeed living in serfdom. They work from eleven and a half to thirteen hours a day for less wages than the average tramp would collect by begging from door to door."

Employment of children in industry was a controversial issue in the early twentieth-century United States, but early efforts to regulate the practice met with little success. In 1877 the Alabama legislature restricted child labor to an eight-hour work day, but this statute was repealed in 1895 at the behest of an executive who had moved his mill down from New England. When the Supreme Court struck down legislative efforts to curb the practice and Congress presented a constitutional amendment allowing child-labor regulation, southern textile interests joined the National Association of Manufacturers in opposing the amendment. One southern political leader condemned the proposal as "a fiendish scheme laid in foreign countries." Another

charged: "It would destroy the home. It would destroy a civilization based on the Bible." Such opposition delayed federal restrictions on child labor until the New Deal years, but employers and
state legislators gradually bowed to mounting public pressure. Between 1914 and 1930 the percentage of textile workers under sixteen
years of age declined from 15 percent to less than 4 percent, and
all the southern states took steps to prevent employment of persons
under fourteen. Still, some mills circumvented the minimum age re-
quirement by allowing young children to "help out" other family
members, thereby augmenting the family income and training
themselves for what was likely to become their life's work. In 1974
a female textile employee who first went into the mill in 1917 at age
eight remembered: "I never started getting paid until I was twelve
years old. I'd go in at 6:30 and work until 8, getting to school just
in time to get in line; I'd come after school and work until 6, then
I'd come in on Saturday and work until 12."

The minimum age for employment in the mills determined the
amount of formal education most mill village children received because most were forced to leave school when they were old enough
to be employed. One long-time mill employee remembered sadly,
"I finished eighth grade . . . and I never got to go back. . . . I cried
for two weeks, I wanted to go to school so bad, but back then times
were hard."

One of the most controversial practices among textile mill oper-
ators was the maintenance of a company store where employees
bought goods, often on credit, and often at exorbitant prices. In some
cases workers received only scrip, redeemable at the company store.
Such stores were less common by the 1920s, but as late as 1937 a
Collier's reporter discovered several and produced evidence that some
mill workers were still being held in what amounted to debt peonage.
A number of mill hands showed pay vouchers documenting the fact
that after deductions for bills at the company store, the employee
was entitled to no pay whatsoever for his or her week's work.

By the mid-1920s southern mill workers also had to contend with
the "Bedeaux" or "stretch out" system introduced by efficiency experts to lower labor costs and raise productivity. The system
amounted to an attempt to apply New England time unit productivity standards to employees whose hours were much longer, and

workers saw the new expectations as an attempt to get more labor out of them for less money. In many instances failure to meet arbitrary quotas resulted in a sudden reduction in an employee's wage. At best, the stress of meeting these heavier demands could induce migraine headaches and send a mill-employed female home to have "a good cry," or her husband off on a drinking binge. At worst, the system could produce severe economic abuses, like those at the Hattiesburg, Mississippi, factory where experienced workers toiled nine hours to earn five hours' pay and where one female employee earned 97 cents for two weeks' work. Gastonia, North Carolina, textile workers parodied the stretch-out by holding a parade featuring eight men carrying a coffin bearing a body representing the mill superintendent. At periodic intervals the superintendent's "corpse" would sit upright and yell, "Six Can Do It!"

Stressful labor left its mark on mill workers. Wilbur J. Cash provided this description of the typical mill worker: "A dead-white skin, a sunken chest, and stooping shoulders were the earmarks of the breed. Chinless faces, microcephalic foreheads, rabbit teeth, goggling deadfish eyes, rickety limbs and stunted bodies abounded— over and beyond the limit of their prevalence in the countryside. The women were characteristically stringy-haired and limp of breast at twenty, and shrunken hags at thirty or forty." So pervasive was this stereotype of mill workers that patent medicines were even developed to cure it. David Carlton discovered an advertisement for "Hop bitters" manufactured especially to rid operatives of "pallid faces, poor appetite, languid, miserable feelings, poor blood, inactive liver, kidney and urinary troubles."

Next to its blacks, the South's mill people were perceived as its most pitiable and oppressed residents. Most of the region's textile workers were in-migrants from surrounding rural areas. Hence, especially in the late nineteenth century, life in the villages had a distinctly rural flavor. Residents nostalgically designated the seasons with farm-derived references—"hog killin' weather" or "laying by time"—and mill villagers who missed the independence and periodic leisure of farm life often gathered to swap yarns about the past. In the late nineteenth century, millhands hunted and fished to supplement their meager diets. As time passed such activities became more recreational but remained popular, in part because they afforded an opportunity to reassert rural ties.

Farm-born mill workers who were heads of households reflected so wistfully on their pasts not only because they missed their friends and kin back on the farm but also because they could not escape the haunting feeling that they had failed as farmers. Although most who moved into mill work apparently had little choice if they were to hope for a better future economically, the loss of individuality and the tendency for their fellow southerners to regard farming, even sharecropping, as a more respectable pursuit than mill work left many mill villagers with shattered self-concepts. Many formerly independent farmers saw themselves as prisoners in an industrial environment. As Ben Robertson noted in his *Red Hills and Cotton*: "We ourselves got up before daylight, but there was something alarming in being ordered to rise by a factory whistle. It was the command that frightened, the imperative in the note. . . . I thought it was terrible to spend six days of every week in a mill. I had never spent all of a day in any house in my life." Many of those who remained on the farm dismissed mill workers as people who were simply "sorry" and had not been industrious enough to "make a go" of farming. Those who lived near a mill village also disparaged "lint heads," asserting that they were uncouth, dirty, and ignorant, and worst of all seemed to lack the desire to be otherwise. Mill wives were seldom welcome in the town's middling society and almost never in higher strata. Mill children and town children might attend school together, but as adolescence and the "dating age" approached, social pressures pulled them apart, in much the same way that black and white playmates were separated as they grew older. Also, as with blacks, there was a tendency for local law-enforcement officials to regard the village's "internal" crimes as less worthy of investigation. Many mill villagers responded to the prejudices they faced by keeping unto themselves and venturing into the nearby town only when absolutely necessary. Their isolation may have fostered a sense of community among the mill folk, but it also bred in them an intense provincialism that further marked them as "different" from their fellow southerners.

Clarence Cason recalled the mill workers as a solitary, downtrodden lot:

Their shoulders and arms dragged with obvious weariness; soiled lint from the mills hung on their clothing and in their hair. They walked along in single file without talking to each other, about three paces apart, going to town on Saturday afternoon. Now and then we would encounter them in some of the grocery stores. Mainly they seemed to buy snuff and stick candy but the clerks never paid much attention to them one way or the other. They were just the cotton mill people. The clerks often asked them to wait while customers were being attended to, and the cotton mill people never seemed to mind.

The psychic scars inflicted by their circumstances often had a lasting effect on mill folk, such as the woman who admitted that "Even to this day [1975], I do not like to tell anyone that I ever worked in a mill."

Although there were some signs of self-pity, many mill workers refused to blame their employers for their difficulties. Expectations were low and humility encouraged, and most workers tried to take setbacks in stride. Raised on religious fundamentalism, mill workers were inclined to believe that the events that shaped their lives were "in God's hands." A worker steeped in the doctrine of original sin was likely to attribute his misfortunes to his own misdeeds.

Although David McCarn's "Cotton Mill Colic" appeared to express resentment, its overall tone was one of resignation:

When you go to work, you work like the devil
At the end of the week you're not on the level
Pay day comes, you pay your rent
When you get through, you've not got a cent
To buy fat back meat and pinto beans
Now and then you get turnip greens
No use to colic, we're all that way
Can't get the money to move away
I'm a-gonna starve, everybody will
'Cause you can't make a livin' at a cotton mill.[1]

Most cotton mill employees voiced few public complaints because they felt they were much better off in the cotton mills than they

---

[1] "Cotton Mill Colic" by David McCarn, © 1930, by Peer International Corporation. Copyright renewed.

would have been in the cotton fields. Even at $2.50 per week a late nineteenth-century worker was earning considerably more than he was accustomed to making as a sharecropper. Despite occasional vows to do so, relatively few mill workers ever returned to the farm permanently. As the generations passed, children of mill workers expressed less and less desire to return to agricultural pursuits. By the end of World War II, workers earning $40 per week could console themselves with the fact that such an income was far greater than what they could reasonably expect to earn on the farm. Moreover, mill housing had improved considerably, and more companies were offering such fringe benefits as insurance, recreational programs for youth, and even vacation cabins at the beach.

Mill workers gave up many of the advantages of farm life, but they also enjoyed many benefits not available on the farm. Ben Robertson recalled the autumn afternoon his aunt and uncle had spent with a tenant farmer agonizing over the latter's decision to leave the farm. After the distraught tenant finally ended his debate with himself by declaring: "I'm ambitious, and I'm strong. I'm going to do it," he packed his family into a wagon and moved into a nearby mill village. Robertson neatly summarized the pluses and minuses of this decision: "The whistle blew for them at half past four o'clock and at six their work started. Six to six was their shift. It was a hard life for a family accustomed to the open, but Saturday was payday— every Saturday." For this family, at least, the mill produced a more materially prosperous existence and a more attractive future for their descendants: "They bought a new coal stove with their cash money. They bought an icebox, a car, a radio. Mr. Tom's oldest boy eventually was graduated from college."

As the twentieth century progressed, textile manufacturers and other executives gradually abandoned the construction of mill villages, choosing instead to put their new factories in rural areas or in sites surrounded by a pool of cheap, eager, and antiunion rural labor. Because of this locational pattern, workers were able to retain their rural residences and ties even as they moved into the world of industry. Even plants that located in larger towns and cities paid close attention to the labor available in the countryside and often showed a preference for workers drawn from outlying rural areas. In 1930, for example, Goodyear Tire and Rubber responded to the warmly pro-business climate in Gadsden, Alabama, by choosing that city for a large plant. Ironically, company officials had also been impressed by the highly individualistic residents of the nearby Sand Mountain area who seemed the unlikeliest candidates for unionization imaginable. Local job applicants were soon saying that "you had to live on Sand Mountain or cross it in order to get a job with Goodyear." When a new employee reported for work he was bluntly reminded, "There's a barefoot boy (from Sand Mountain) waiting at the gate for your job."

Industrialization strengthened local economies not only by creating new jobs but through the "spinoff" of positions in related industries or supporting services stimulated by economic growth. Studies of rural industrialization showed that the employment "multiplier effect," while lower than most experts theorized, was often as much as three to one (three new jobs in industry were responsible for one new job in services, retail, or other pursuits). Many rural areas failed to benefit fully from the multiplier effect because new plants were staffed by a surplus of agricultural labor from the surrounding countryside, so industrial growth did not necessarily result in a significant population influx. Moreover, many workers lived some distance from the plant and spent much of their income outside the economic sphere in which they worked.

In a typical Tennessee plant, workers commuted an average distance of nearly ten miles, and more than 20 percent drove over fifteen. In 1958 more than 15 percent of a Star City, Arkansas, plant's work force travelled at least thirty miles to their jobs each day. For the most part employees were willing to accept the expense and inconvenience of commuting in order to remain on their farms, and often continue to farm. Ironically, by the late 1950s, industrial employment had become the only means by which rural residents could continue to cope with the shrinking buying power of their farm incomes. By working early mornings, late afternoons or evenings, or by seeking night shift employment, farmers could still work a crop while earning an industrial paycheck. Government crop reduction programs made life easier for worker/farmers by encouraging them to plant modest acreages in order to receive "diversion" payments for land they agreed not to cultivate.

Farmers who took jobs in a new plant in a rural area did not always see a dramatic improvement in their circumstances, especially if the plant's wages were relatively low and agriculture continued to dominate the local economy. The opening of the Jackson Furniture Company plant, which employed 130 persons in Chickasaw County, Mississippi, brought economic advancement to some local residents, but a 1963 study concluded that "living levels are still relatively low and not appreciably higher for the factory worker than for the farmer."

The Chickasaw County example notwithstanding, the economic impact of industrial growth on the rural South was largely positive. Almost all available case studies of rural industrialization showed significant improvements in the levels of living of new employees. In the mid-1950s nearly 70 percent of a Virginia factory's work force claimed they had purchased their homes since coming to work at the plant. Industrial employment brought automobiles, modern appliances, and a host of other conveniences that once had been only items on the "wish list." For example, as of 1958, nearly 24 percent of the Star City plant's workers had purchased a television set since going to work in industry.

A study of the impact of a new mill employing nearly 300 people in rural Charlotte County, Virginia, between 1949 and 1954 demonstrated that industrialization had apparently spurred diversification of both agriculture and industry. Per capita income rose by more than 15 percent. Twenty new retail stores appeared and retail sales rose by 50 percent. The mill failed to halt black out-migration from Charlotte County, but the white exodus slowed and the white population began to increase. Overall levels of living rose significantly—26 percent of the county's families were supplied with electricity for the first time, 8 percent got their first telephones, and 9 percent their first automobiles. The same period saw the number of rural families owning motor vehicles rise by 10 percent so that 75 percent of these families owned automobiles in 1954, as compared to 77 percent of the families living in town.

Income differentials between farmers and industrial workers were striking. In Allegheny County, North Carolina, a 1966 survey showed wage earner incomes ranging from $2,500 to $3,500 while average incomes for farms supporting entire families stood at only $3,000 annually. Even those rural residents who did not work in the factory appeared to benefit from industrial expansion. The prospect of a steady and relatively sizable pay check drew farm operators (especially operators of smaller farms) off the land. Thus, although total farm income continued to shrink, it was often being divided among fewer farmers, many of whom had expanded their holdings by purchasing or renting the land of those who accepted factory employment. The only major objection which farmers appeared to have to industrial growth was the fact that it tended to reduce the supply of agricultural labor. "You can't get anybody to work for you anymore," was a standard complaint in industrializing areas, but the problem for cash poor farmers was not so much a labor shortage as a slow but steady rise in their labor costs. Between 1953 and 1958, for example, farm wages in areas like industrializing Lawrence County, Tennessee, rose from $3.50 per day to $5.00 per day.

Although the opening of a large plant usually signalled impressive gains in statistical measures of economic growth, underdeveloped areas found themselves dependent on and often dominated by a single large employer. The most extreme form of such dependence was the "company town." Elizabeth, Louisiana, began in 1906 as the property of the Industrial Lumber Company, whose sawmill was the only local industry until 1926, when a paper mill came to town. After World War II, control of the mill and the town fell into the hands of the paper mill owner, C. G. McGehee, who first leased it and then bought it outright in 1955. McGehee owned houses, streets, and facilities as well as the two mills that provided the community's only payrolls. Elizabeth had neither mayor, city council, nor police, and depended on McGehee for its entire governance. McGehee, who continued to live in Jacksonville, Florida, flew into Elizabeth periodically to insure that his interests were being served and protected. Elizabeth remained a company town until 1964, when its first mayor and board of aldermen took office.

The Tennessee Copper Company's Copperhill, Tennessee, copper-sulfuric acid operations were the staff of life of relatively remote southeastern Tennessee and adjoining counties of Georgia and North Carolina. Company employees received wages considerably higher than average for any of the three states. In addition to hiring more than 2,500 people with an average annual payroll of $12 million, the company also spent $6 million for local goods and services by the early 1970s. Still, with a large number of workers coming in from other counties, unemployment remained a problem in Polk County. In other labor-surplus areas of the South, low-wage industries had moved in to take advantage of a large worker pool, but garment and textile firms were reluctant to pit themselves against a higher paying competitor for employees. Lacking sufficient opportunities in other industries, Polk County continued to lose population, despite the higher-than-average wage dispensed by the Tennessee Copper Company.

Large, dominating employers were often in a position to keep other industries out of their area. Critics insisted that Cannon Mills had often managed to refuse entree to other employers interested in the Kannapolis, North Carolina, area. The same charge was leveled against the Tennessee Copper Company by a local community development organization chairman. In a plea for help from the Tennessee Division for Industrial Development, this local booster noted that except for a tiny garment plant employing twenty-five workers, his efforts to bring in industry had been fruitless. He claimed that "we have in the past had a lot of opposition from the copper company when we tried to get some kind of industry to locate here." With a sizable labor surplus and an average of seventy-five students graduating from the local high school annually, out-migration was likely to continue. The frustrated Polk County resident concluded that local youth had little choice but "to leave the state or county to gain employment after we pay our taxes and educate them here they have to leave it simply don't make sense to me."

Communities dominated by a single industry often enjoyed only limited gains, but the gradual diversification of local industry could produce expanded opportunities, especially for the sons and daughters of the workers in a low-wage plant. Alamance County, North Carolina, provided a useful example. From a modest beginning in the nineteenth century, the area became a textile and hosiery manufacturing center and remained so until shortly after World War II, when a Western Electric facility opened in Burlington. By 1959 the plant's work force had grown to 4,000, about 10 percent of the local population. At this point approximately 31 percent of local white males worked in textiles as compared to 17 percent in electrical machinery production. A survey of local workers suggested that the textile work force was drawn directly from the farm while the blue-collar workers in the electrical industry were often the sons of textile workers. The Burlington experience showed that if a local industrial economy became more diversified, over a period of three generations a farm-born son might move into textile employment only to have his children step up into a better paying, more promising career in electrical machinery. Electrical workers showed a more pronounced pattern of upward mobility than did their textile worker fathers. Presumably the offspring of these younger workers would, with proper training, be able to compete for some of the managerial positions initially filled by in-migrants.

Although its economic impact was generally beneficial, industrialization posed a number of social and psychological problems for rural residents in the post-World War II period. Many new plants sought an exclusively female work force. In a Star City, Arkansas, plant 89 percent of the employees were female. If work assignments did not require heavy lifting or if they involved sewing or other traditionally "female" tasks, hiring women made sense. Females could be paid less than males (on the grounds that they were supplementing their husbands' income), and were even less likely to complain about working conditions or listen to the entreaties of union recruiters. In communities like Natchez, Mississippi, the underemployment of males became so severe that industrial promoters set their sights on firms that would hire men as a means of offsetting a local concentration of female-employing plants. The continuing preference of many new plants for a female work force denied many husbands their traditional roles as breadwinners, especially if declining incomes forced them to abandon farming. Many men drifted into a role disparagingly referred to as that of a "go-getter"— so dubbed because he rose promptly at 4:45 each weekday afternoon from his seat on a soft-drink crate at the country store and sheepishly declared, "Well, boys, it's time to go get her." At this point, he departed to pick up his wife as her work day ended at the local garment plant.

The "working wife" was just that. Not only did she have to cope with the demands of her job but she was normally expected to continue to meet the general responsibilities associated with being a farm wife. Canned goods and new appliances helped with cooking and cleaning (one of the most monstrous evils that industrialization inflicted on the rural South was the introduction of canned biscuits), but summer brought gardening and canning, and winter the inevitable preoccupation with hogkilling—"working up" the sausage, making the lard, cooking the "cracklins" and, of course, cleaning the "chittlins." If the cotton got grassy, Saturdays could be spent wielding a hoe, and during grain-cutting season nights were often spent preparing the next day's meals for "the hands." Although the factory seemed to offer an escape from the drudgery of farm life, it all too often simply increased the wife's workload. Her role as breadwinner did not relieve her of her duties as breadmaker, laundress, and mother.

Male heads of household who went into the factory in the post-World War II years faced an adjustment that was in many ways more difficult than the one experienced by their late nineteenth-century predecessors. By the postwar period many of the South's industrial workers had no farm background whatever. Experienced in factory work, they often regarded with amusement the older and less educated farmers who had finally given up on agriculture. The factory of the 1950s and 1960s was a more complex and pressured environment than the nineteenth-century cotton mill had been. Older, inexperienced workers who could easily pick two hundred pounds of cotton a day often found it difficult to keep up on the assembly line, and regarded with fearful contempt the machines which tyrannized them and occasionally chopped off their fingers. A body that had once worked from sunup to sundown often seemed exhausted at the end of a tense eight-hour shift. Such workers found it difficult to feel comfortable in their new surroundings and obviously longed for the days of independence in the fields when they had worked hard but at their own pace.

As traumatic as it may have been, most southern blacks probably would have jumped at the chance to obtain factory employment. For the most part black workers found themselves shut out from even the slender benefits of industrialization that trickled down to white southern labor. No employer was more consistent in its discrimination against blacks than the textile industry. As of 1920, for example, less than 5 percent of North Carolina's textile work force was black. Between 1918 and 1950 blacks fell from 9 to 4.8 percent of the textile work force in South Carolina. Even the prosperity of World War II helped little. In South Carolina's textile mills the drop in white male employment due to military service or the attraction of more lucrative defense industry jobs was offset by a corresponding increase in the employment not of blacks but of white females. When blacks were hired, they seldom were involved in the actual production process. In 1919 the president of Dan River Mills remarked: "As regards colored people, we only employ them as sweepers, scourers, truck drivers, and in the dye-house and picker rooms. We do not have them in the mill proper, except in . . . menial capacities." Eighty-seven percent of blacks in southern cotton mills were classified as laborers. Black women swept, scrubbed, and cleaned trash from cotton; black men unloaded and "broke" the bales and fired the boilers. A 1952 survey asserted that there was not a single black weaver, spinner, or loom fixer among the 400,000 textile workers in Virginia and the Carolinas.

Limited opportunities in the textile industry encouraged blacks to flee areas of high textile concentration. On the surface the textile industry's refusal to hire blacks in significant numbers appeared to be contrary to the industry's economic best interest. Blacks were the cheapest of the South's cheap labor and thus were the logical work force for an industry where labor costs were crucial. On the other hand, white resistance would probably have blocked any large-scale industrial employment of blacks. At any rate, so long as blacks provided a large, underutilized labor pool, whites were in no position to agitate for better wages or working conditions. As a result, even with blacks shut out of the textile industry, employers were able to pay wages much lower than those paid in New England textile mills.

The tendency of textile employers to seek areas with a large surplus of white labor combined with the tendency of blacks to move from textile to non-textile areas to create a significant economic development imbalance. The counties with large textile payrolls became relatively more prosperous (at least in terms of aggregate and individual economic statistics) while areas with fewer nonagricultural opportunities had to absorb an influx of blacks who contributed to already sizable and impoverished labor surpluses. White resistance to black employment in textiles not only contributed to an uneven pattern of growth, it also prevented textile employers from following a natural tendency to hire the cheapest labor available, possibly slowing further the growth of what was already a "slow-growth" industry.

Discrimination was hardly confined to the textile industry. Prior to the 1960s the advocates of industrialization made little effort to provide jobs for blacks except in cases where incoming industries required labor so arduous and distasteful as to be unattractive to whites. Community leaders and manufacturers reached a tacit understanding that industrial jobs were normally for whites only, leaving blacks as an ample supply of low-cost agricultural labor. Even Henry Ford, whose plants outside the South were generally integrated, employed no southern blacks prior to 1940. When blacks did find employment in southern industries they were restricted to the most menial, least rewarding jobs. Often the skill levels of their new jobs were no higher than those they performed on the farm or on the logging crew. Nor were prospects for advancement that much brighter. As late as the end of the 1960s, 87 percent of southern black workers held blue-collar jobs. No major southern industry employed more than 2.6 percent of its black workers in white-collar occupations. For black females the situation was even worse—well over half the women workers in southern paper, lumber, and tobacco facilities were "service" employees engaged in cleaning and maintenance of buildings.

Although it represented a definite improvement over farm work, industrial employment was often a cruelly frustrating experience for southern blacks, who were seldom accorded the benefits of seniority or expertise when decisions about promotion or retention were being made. Salary discrimination was blatant. In one Louisiana plant studied at the end of the 1950s, 20 percent of all employees earned $45.00 per week, but only 2 percent of black workers were paid at this rate. Because blacks often filled the unskilled "hard labor" jobs, they were most susceptible to displacement by automation. Contrary to expectations, unionization was no boon to southern blacks. Many unions, like their employer adversaries, accommodated themselves to local racial custom. In the southern coal fields, the advent of unionization actually appeared to trigger a decline in the percentage of blacks employed. The salary demands of the United Mine Workers apparently encouraged the mechanization which cost many black miners their jobs, and the UMW took little action to remedy the situation. Many unions in the South ended their actively discriminatory policies only in the face of federal pressure in the 1960s.

Federal insistence on nondiscriminatory hiring aided blacks considerably, but many firms simply avoided locations with heavy concentrations of blacks. Even in the 1970s the best hope for black progress remained the "trickle-down" benefits of accelerated industrial growth which caused whites to vacate lower paying jobs for more lucrative opportunities in new industries. Black movement into the textile industry was a case in point. Low-wage textile mills could not compete with the better-paying industries that appeared in the 1960s and 1970s, so blacks were able to move into the jobs abandoned by whites. Expanded vocational training programs also promised to upgrade the skill levels of southern blacks and liberate them from the region's underemployed agricultural surplus, although initially these programs still funneled blacks into the least remunerative jobs created by southern industrial growth.

The case of South Carolina blacks in the 1960s suggested significant but still limited progress. During the decade the percentage of the state's blacks working in manufacturing doubled while the percentage of whites employed increased by only 17 percent. The most striking gains were made by black women, whose representation in the manufacturing work force rose from 4 to 23 percent. Almost half the state's ten-year gains in manufacturing employment belonged to blacks who were moving into the poorly paying textile and textile-related jobs vacated by whites who moved up to more lucrative ones.

Frustrating as it was, the struggle by blacks to gain a foothold in southern industry occasionally produced a personal success story. In 1969 the *New York Times* provided an account of a black former sharecropper with five years of education who moved into textile employment in 1965, beginning with menial tasks but rising within four years to the traditionally "white" position of loom fixer. The former sharecropper purchased a seventy-eight acre farm, where he worked after hours and built a new, fully carpeted house. After four years his $13,000 income was nearly quadruple the figure he had earned before entering the mill. Moreover, sharecropping was not only not a part of his children's future, it now seemed a remote part of their past. A daughter was in secretarial school and a son had just won a four-year scholarship to college.

Just as most black workers found it difficult to claim an equitable share of the benefits of industrial growth, union organizers faced frustration at every turn as they tried to rally southern labor to the banner of collective bargaining. Cheap, nonunion labor remained the key element of the sales pitch to new industry throughout the post-Reconstruction century. Promises of "long hours at low wages" gradually evolved into "a day's work for a day's pay," but whatever euphemisms they chose, development spokesmen seemed to have few qualms about peddling a surplus of cheap workers. Mississippi's especially desperate quest for new industry led developers to make dollars-and-cents calculations showing Magnolia State workers to be "dirt cheap" even in comparison to unskilled laborers in the nearby states of Alabama and Louisiana. Like many other states, Mississippi's ads rationalized the meager wages paid its workers by emphasizing that most of them were rural farm folk who supplemented their incomes and diets by farming and gardening and therefore needed less income than the average industrial laborer.

The nonunion message evolved from a gleeful "No Unions Here!" to a somber assertion that a state's or community's workers were too grateful for their jobs and too much imbued with a sense of "fair play" and loyalty to forsake their employers for some "outsider." A high percentage of southern workers were "native born Anglo Saxon" and far too individualistic to succumb to the gospel of collectivism.

For the most part industrial developers could deliver on their promises where nonunion labor was concerned. Although the National Labor Union made some small-scale recruiting efforts in the South in the late 1860s, the Noble Order of the Knights of Labor was the first union to have significant impact before the 1880s. The secret of the Knights' appeal was their willingness to accept all who toiled (except lawyers, bankers, gamblers, and liquor dealers). As the nation began to recover from the Panic of 1873, the Knights dispatched fifteen organizers to launch what became the South's first organizing drive. By 1883 the organization had locals in every southern state except North Carolina and Florida. Much of the Knights' activity was concentrated in urban centers, but the group was also active in rural areas where disgruntled agrarians were displaying a surprising propensity to organize. The Knights also had several locals comprised of coal miners and lumber workers, but made little headway among employees of the region's emerging textile industry. The union was also active politically, taking credit for the election of several mayors and congressmen. In the long run, however, in the South the Knights were less a strong labor union than a mass movement that resembled the agrarian protest organizations of the late 1880s. Although emotionally inspiring, their open arms appeal to all who toiled made it difficult for the Knights of Labor to build the tightly knit organization they needed to survive in the unfriendly environment of the late nineteenth-century South.

It remained for the American Federation of Labor to consolidate the South's scattered locals into a relatively cohesive union movement. The AFL made its most rapid strides at the end of the 1880s as southern industry began a phase of rapid expansion. This growth continued into the 1890s and by 1919 every state had a federation of labor, with organizers at work in at least 173 cities.

As in the rest of the nation, the pattern of union growth in the South was one of trickle-down expansion from the more to the lesser skilled occupations. During World War I, economic expansion, labor shortages, and a relatively favorable federal attitude stimulated union growth, but the postwar economic slump of 1920-21 proved extremely damaging to union efforts. The United Textile Workers had made some significant gains during the war, but the union was powerless as employers facing competitive pressure in a slumping economy cut work forces and wages drastically. A disastrous strike involving 9,000 North Carolina textile workers in 1921 effectively crippled the textile union movement in the South just as employers began to exhibit new militance in their determination to defy the unions. The "Open Shop" movement won support from politicians, boosters, and journalists throughout the South, and individual workers could only issue feeble complaints in the face of further wage cuts and increased work loads.

As the 1920s came to an end the South's textile workers made several last-gasp attempts to recover the gains they had lost during the decade. In Elizabethton, Tennessee, 550 young women walked off their jobs (which paid them an average of $8.96 per week), setting off a siege of violence and intimidation. On the heels of the Elizabethton uproar came the revolt at the Loray Mill in Gastonia, North Carolina. Initially workers rebelled specifically against pay cuts and work-load increases, but after the involvement of the Communist-backed National Textile Workers Union, workers extended their goals to include minimum weekly wages of $20.00 and equal pay for women and children. Such demands seemed outrageous to many residents, most of whom were already hostile to the idea of Communist activity in Gastonia. Still, a core of strikers persisted amidst scattered violence (including the shooting death of the local police chief) until a mob broke up a caravan of strikers with a hail of gunfire. Labor violence reached a peak in the South in the years 1934-35, when at least forty-two workers and organizers were killed.

Strikes and blatant examples of worker abuse helped to call attention to the plight of southern labor, but it was not until the Great Depression and the subsequent federal effort to stimulate economic recovery that unions could point to lasting gains in the South. The cause of organized labor received a much-needed boost when New Deal labor measures appeared to put the White House's stamp of approval on union membership. The National Industrial Recovery Act encouraged those inclined to bargain collectively, and although NIRA fell at the hands of the Supreme Court, labor got another boost from the 1935 National Labor Relations Act, which promised protection and established the National Labor Relations Board to insure that workers received fair treatment.

Despite such encouragement, progress in recruiting new members remained slow. If unions were ever to have a significant impact on the South, the region's textile and garment plants would have to be conquered, no small accomplishment considering the fact that these operations were often small, widely dispersed in rural areas, and staffed primarily by females. By the end of the 1930s, the International Ladies Garment Workers could claim fewer than 1,000 members below the Mason-Dixon line. The CIO's 1946 "Operation Dixie" organizing drive proved to be a disappointment, although union membership in the South grew nearly 40 percent faster than the national rate between 1939 and 1953. Still, in 1964 the percentage of the South's nonagricultural labor force affiliated with unions was only 50 percent of the nonsouthern average, roughly the same relative position it had occupied in 1939. Despite the rapid growth of the region's industry in the decades that followed, southern union membership grew so slowly that by 1976 only slightly more than 14 percent of the region's nonfarm workers had been unionized as compared to a nearly 25 percent average nationwide. Had it not been for the influence of the United Mine Workers in Kentucky, southern membership totals would have been even more anemic. In neither of the two Carolinas, for example, could labor organizations claim as much as 7 percent of the nonagricultural work force.

Union sympathizers once hoped that the southward migration of large firms whose northern employees were unionized would foster a more receptive environment for collective bargaining. By the 1970s, however, even companies like General Motors were beginning to respond to increased competition by trying to capitalize on the dollar-per-hour-plus wage differentials that could be maintained at non-union operations in Alabama, Georgia, and Mississippi. Only one of the ten General Motors plants opened in the South between 1973 and 1978 was unionized at the end of 1978.

Nonunion companies naturally had a vested interest in maintaining a nonunion environment. Jonathan Daniels once charged that Southern employers had blocked unionization by using "everything from holiness preachers to rednecked deputy sheriffs, from the Bible to the bull whip." Union representatives clearly agreed with Daniels's pronouncement. They cited examples like that of the Sewall Manufacturing Company of Bremen, Georgia, which mailed employees a picture of a union leader dancing with the wife of a black diplomat. Union spokesmen also charged that the Trane Company of Clarksville, Tennessee, distributed two paychecks to workers prior to a union election, one of them purported to represent the amount of union dues to be deducted from employee paychecks should the work force vote to organize. Elsewhere, textile magnate Roger Milliken showed himself to be a man of his word when he made good on his threat to close his company's Darlington, South Carolina, plant rather than submit to unionization.

The widespread resistance of southern employers to labor unions is better understood in the light of the region's heavy concentration of competitive industries for whom labor costs were crucial. Whereas large firms in noncompetitive industries might find it possible to pass the increasing labor costs spurred by unionization on to consumers, textile, apparel, and other firms whose operating costs were not necessarily transferrable considered it worth the effort to resist unionization as long as possible.

Southern industry's aversion to organized labor was symbolized by the steadfast refusal of the J. P. Stevens Company to enter into meaningful bargaining with its employees. The nation's second largest textile manufacturer, Stevens was first assaulted by the Textile Workers Union of America in 1963. When workers at the company's Roanoke Rapids plants voted for union representation in 1974, labor leaders hoped that a vital crack had been opened in the South's antiunion armor, but it was not until late 1980 that Stevens finally reached a contract agreement with workers at its Roanoke Rapids plants, and even then company representatives made it a point to stress their determination to continue to oppose unionization at other Stevens operations.

Stevens resisted unionism with threats of firings or plant closings and with racially charged suggestions that unionization meant black control in plants where blacks constituted no more than one-third of the work force. When charged by the National Labor Relations Board with such abuses, the company's lawyers used every device available to stall the arbitration process. Stevens officials apparently felt the benefits of resisting unionization outweighed the costs. Between 1965 and 1976 the company was found guilty of fifteen labor law violations for which it was forced, after exhaustive appeals, to pay well over $1 million in damages.

J. P. Stevens' bold defiance of union pressure attracted so much publicity that the firm faced a nationwide consumer boycott in the late 1970s, but local boosters, journalists, and politicians remained steadfast defenders of the company. Stevens' antiunion tactics actually served as models for lawyers and "union-busting" experts who commanded healthy sums to serve as advisors on the matter of maintaining or restoring "the union-free environment." South Carolina's Clemson University even offered textile executives a seminar on the fine points of resisting unionization efforts. Chambers of Commerce spearheaded local resistance to unionization, usually so effectively that during World War II one Danville, Virginia, textile laborer observed wryly that he was "not worried a-tall about the Japs movin' in on us; the Chamber of Commerce has kept unions out, and I reckon as how they can keep the Japs out, too."

Instead of protecting union leaders from lawlessness, community leaders often incited it against them. In Moultrie, Georgia, in 1919, the local Chamber of Commerce convinced farmers that a workers' union at a local packinghouse was a threat to future hog sales. The farmers responded by running the union organizer out of town. In 1922, Harrison, Arkansas, businessmen led a mob that wrecked the union hall of the Brotherhood of Locomotive Engineers. The crowd also stormed the homes of several strikers, whipped them, stripped the clothes from their wives and children, and hung the local machinists' union leader from a local bridge.

The Dallas Chamber of Commerce hinted at the value of the state militia as a strikebreaking force, arguing that Dallas needed a "strong military body" because "conditions might rise at any time which would make the presence here of such a unit highly desirable." Local police often cooperated with antiunion forces by harassing organizers and looking the other way as others harassed, intimidated, and abused them. Many clergymen hoped to defend local employers by branding union organizers as agents of the devil. One minister explained to his flock that the letters "CIO" meant "Christ Is Out."

The local media often contributed a flood of propaganda, such as the none-too-subtle warning, "If you join the CIO, you will be endorsing the closing of a factory." A 1964 organizing campaign at the Monroe Auto Equipment Company Plant in Hartwell, Georgia, led not only to violence but to a bitter antiunion effort by the local media. The town's weekly newspaper warned that Monroe might close its plant if the workers voted for a union. The paper also carried articles charging that UAW President Walter Reuther was a Communist, and linking the UAW to various left-wing and civil rights organizations.

Perhaps no newspaper editor was as consistently and as harshly antiunion in his views as Fred Sullens, who served as editor of the Jackson *Daily News* from 1907 to 1957. Sullens not only linked organized labor to communism but he saw it as a threat to the industrial growth he believed his state so vitally needed: "Strikes and unions don't mix well with the program to get a toe-hold for industry in this commonwealth." Sullens even denied the right of labor to strike, which he likened to "an act of industrial war." He justified the 1919 murder of three union organizers in Bogalusa, Louisiana, with the assertion that it was "better to spill blood in small quantities now than in wholesale quantities later on." Sullens reserved his bitterest contempt for labor leaders such as CIO chief John L.

Lewis, whom he vilified as a would-be dictator, "pig-eyed" and "brute faced," and "far more dangerous than Scarface Al Capone."

Although they often received little protection from harassment, violence, and intimidation, striking workers occasionally retaliated in kind. Such was the case in Elizabeth, Louisiana, where the local paper mills locked out workers threatening to strike in 1952. When the mills reopened and most workers refused to return, the owner of the mill hired scabs to replace strikers, who were also evicted from company housing. With state troopers escorting the scabs, and the guarded, fenced-in plants looking like fortresses, acts of sabotage such as pouring sugar into gas tanks escalated to peppering the homes of scabs with buckshot and ultimately to the use of crude trip bombs constructed of dynamite, fishing line, and rat traps. Although the railroad spur leading to the plant was dynamited, most of the violence was directed against employees loyal to the company. The best measure of the intensity of anti-scab feeling was the fact that Elizabeth's only bar, owned by a plant foreman, was "blown to bits." Still, despite their anger and determination, the strikers were no match for the company, which waited them out for five years, long enough for strikers to find other jobs, or, in some cases, forget what had even caused the strike.

The almost solid front with which the South confronted organized labor had been carefully constructed by political and economic leaders, who insisted that organization posed a mortal threat to efforts to promote industrialization in the region. Southern senators and congressmen were among the most prominent opponents of such pro-labor legislation as the National Labor Relations Act and the Fair Labor Standards Act. State legislators followed the lead of their antiunion congressional counterparts who supported the Taft-Hartley Act in 1947. By 1954 every state in Dixie except Louisiana and Oklahoma had either by statute or constitutional amendment enacted the right-to-work laws which made it illegal for employers to make union membership a prerequisite for employment. At the local level, city councils passed much more restrictive ordinances, requiring unions to pay as much as $2,000 for a license and from $500 to $1,000 for every new member they recruited.

By themselves, propagandizing and intimidation could not have kept the South the bastion of antiunionism it remained. A number of socioeconomic and cultural factors made the southern worker a tough mark for union recruiters. Not the least of these was the average laborer's ignorance of the goals and meaning of unionism. A relatively high degree of functional illiteracy meant that printed material was often of limited value to organizers. Southern workers also knew less about the outside world than their counterparts elsewhere, and their provincial suspicions and hostilities made them susceptible to propaganda like the following: "Who are the men who run this union anyway? . . . Baldenzi, Rieve, Cheepka, Genis, Jabor, Knapik, and Rosenburg. Where do you think these men came from and where do they live? Are their background [sic], upbringing, viewpoints, beliefs, and principles anything like yours and mine?"

Many antiunion advertisements attempted to capitalize on sectional prejudices by charging that unionization drives were part of a Yankee plot to undermine the South's industrial development effort. One Mississippi ad warned: "This election on November 13 will not be just an ordinary union election. For the unions, a victory means they have helped STOP JOBS COMING TO MISSISSIPPI!" Referring to union efforts to halt "runaways"—companies that fled to the South to escape unions—the ad continued: "For many years the UAW and the IUE have been fighting against the creation of jobs in the South and in Mississippi. As far as they're concerned they would just as soon that we were still working in the fields or doing domestic work. As far as they are concerned they would just as soon that we were making $5 per day or unemployed."

The fact that a relatively high percentage of incoming industries located in the South's rural areas also helped to keep union membership low. Rural life had bred a strong sense of individualism, and workers who still lived on the farm thought of themselves as farmers first and workers second. The tendency of southern industries to hire large numbers of females also retarded unionization. Women who worked in factories often did so to supplement their family's farm income and were less likely to express discontent or listen to protest rhetoric. Moreover, women seemed even less informed than their male counterparts about organized labor.

The atmosphere of the "Bible Belt" also helped to insure greater safety from unions because the fundamentalism which flowed from Dixie's pulpits emphasized original sin and God's involvement in all of human affairs and discouraged social activism or class consciousness. Humility was to be prized, one's unworthiness freely admitted. Emphasis on deferred gratification in the hereafter discouraged concern about material progress during one's life on earth. On the other hand, most industrial workers made enough economic progress to convince them that they and their families and descendants were better off in the industrial world than they had been on the farm. Workers bought houses, purchased cars and modern appliances, and generally lived in greater material comfort than their parents had. Was it reasonable, or even "Christian," to expect more? The tendency of fundamentalist religion to encourage acceptance of one's lot in life interacted with the paternalism of the mill owner and the deference which lower-income southern whites had traditionally shown their social and economic superiors. It was hard for the worker to see "Mr. Jim" as an adversary when he had been so kind and understanding in his personal dealings with his employees. Moreover, "Mr. Jim" occupied a position of prominence in the community. How could a mere mill worker challenge him? Historian Melton McLaurin quoted one worker's letter to a potential employer as evidence of these deferential tendencies: "As to pay, you know what the job is worth, and what you can pay for it. It is your work, and I have no rite [sic] to fix it."

Recalling his South Carolina boyhood, Ben Robertson offered this analysis of the millworker's response to his new industrial circumstances and his resistance to unionization:

> In the cotton fields they had conducted their dealings as one independent man with another. Their relationship was individual and personal; and at the mill in town they still were inclined to deal with the overseer as they had with the owner of the cotton field. It still had not fully dawned on these men that the overseer in their mill was not the mill, that he was only an agent. It was still difficult for them to realize that they were not working for any individual as an individual—that they were working for a corporation, complicated and technical and highly organized and involved.

If, despite the propaganda and cultural peculiarities which worked to discourage union sympathies, a southern worker felt inclined to affiliate with a labor organization, he or she had several other factors to consider. As an unskilled or at best semiskilled laborer, the average industrial employee was easily replaced. A steady flow of underemployed agricultural labor fed a labor surplus that denied workers significant leverage when dealing with management. Moreover, union activities were impossible to conceal in small plants and communities. The label of "union man" would be difficult to shed and could mean blacklisting where future employment was concerned. For a worker with a reputation for union sympathies, a decent job might mean moving away from one's community, family, and friends.

Developers insisted that resistance to unionization was a keystone of their efforts to bring economic prosperity to the South, citing the contentions of neoclassical economists that continued industrial growth would one day bring the earnings of southern labor in line with those of workers elsewhere in the nation. Few of the region's political and economic leaders came to grips, however, with the question of how wage rates were to be equalized so long as they worked to preserve conditions favoring differentials. In fact, for most of the twentieth century, wage discrepancies remained relatively constant, with southern wages standing at 86 percent of the national average in 1907 and in approximately the same position in 1945. In the next fifteen years wage rates in Dixie varied between twenty and twenty-five percentage points below the national average. Many southern workers in isolated, low-wage plants actually fell even farther below the national mean in the postwar period. In 1963 apparel workers in North Carolina earned only $1.39 per hour as compared to the $2.01 hourly wage paid their New York counterparts. In addition to the South's unfavorable industry mix, low levels of union membership appeared to be the key to interregional wage variations. A 1977 survey showed a wage differential of from 18 to 22 percent between union and nonunion members in the South Central states. Not only were southern wages lower, but fringe benefits were also less attractive. Disability payments were smaller and available over a shorter duration than elsewhere. Paid vacations were more of a rarity. Critics charged that large-scale unionization might eliminate such discrepancies, but southern leaders remained adamant in their opposition to unions.

Some economists who took a different view of antiunion policies also took a different view of regional wage differentials. Contrary to economic theory, the growth of southern industry had not resulted in equalization of wage rates. Hence even in the 1970s the region continued to appeal to investors on the basis of lower labor costs, and many economists insisted that such cost advantages were essential to further growth. According to such a view union growth might, just as development leaders warned, undermine efforts to promote future expansion. Certainly a company seeking to minimize its labor costs would be more likely to locate in a nonunion area than in one where a substantial portion of the work force was organized. Relocating industrialists clearly approved of the paradoxical efforts of southern leaders to improve the region's overall economic status by avoiding conditions that might create pressure for higher wages for southern workers.

In well over a century of assaults on the South's mills and factories, union leaders found that persistence was no guarantee of success. On the other hand, the limited victories they enjoyed are more significant when viewed in terms of the political, cultural, and economic obstacles they confronted at every turn. Defenders of the southern status quo perceived the labor threat as a genuine impediment to the recruitment of low-wage industry. In addition, efforts to organize southern workers endangered the principal elements of the orthodoxy that sustained socioeconomic and political stability in the post-Reconstruction South. Unionization raised not only the specter of redistribution of wealth but the possibility of class conflict significant enough to encourage insurgent white workers to reconsider their traditional antagonism toward blacks.

The long-term implications of a sizable union presence in the South encouraged southern leaders to treat organized labor as a more immediate threat than it ever became. In fact, the exaggerated response of political and industrial leaders to the onslaughts of union organizers presented a classic example of the manner in which the crusade for economic change often served as a vehicle for social and political continuity. In the propaganda of development leaders, organized labor became an enemy to both progress and tradition, threatening simultaneously to rob the South of its future and to undermine a way of life deeply rooted in its past.

Although there was perceptible improvement from generation to generation, a century after the New South Crusade began in earnest, southern wage earners remained the poorest paid, most under-benefited industrial workers in the United States. Interregional wage differentials contributed to their continuing relative economic deprivation but were an important factor in the effort to provide them with expanded industrial employment opportunities in the future. Charges of exploitation notwithstanding, most southern industrial workers were unwilling to jeopardize their improved standards of living and prospects for continued gains by leaving the factory or mobilizing to improve wages and working conditions. Thus, although the South's persistent appeal to low wage, nonunion industry came in for mounting criticism in the Sunbelt era, surprisingly little of this criticism came from the workers themselves.

5. Industrial Development and Reform in the Post-World War II South

Even in the Sunbelt era, most southern industries maintained their labor orientation, but much of the growth of the post-World War II period had resulted from the expansion of better-paying, faster-growing industries whose managers and executives expected more from a plant location than access to cheap labor. In order to attract investments from these more desirable firms, states and communities were expected to support social and political reforms as well as improvements in public facilities and institutions. Moreover, the managers and executives of these firms would presumably insist on continuing efforts to improve the quality of life at the local and state level. Thus more rapid economic progress seemed both dependent on and supportive of efforts to promote reform in the South.

Observers had long insisted that the real solutions to the South's economic problems were not solely economic but social, political, and institutional as well. Writing in 1960, William H. Nicholls argued that the South's slow growth rate was closely related to a number of regional deficiencies including the persistence of agrarian values, a rigid social hierarchy, an undemocratic political structure, a generally weak concept of social responsibility, and extreme conformity of thought and behavior.

Nicholls attributed these deficiencies to the persistence of the rigid rural substructure that dominated southern society even in the post-World War II period. He stressed the absence of an independent middle class whose values would have challenged the traditionalism that held the South back. He attributed the absence of a dynamic bourgeoisie to "the glacial slowness of southern urbanization," the persistence of antiurban political structures, the rural and small-town character of much of southern industry, and the absence of a challenge to the existing middle class from the low-income, working-class population. For Nicholls and others a self-reinforcing principle emerged—a social and political environment more reflective of middle-class values would result in more rapid growth, which in turn would produce a social and political environment more compatible with middle-class values. As used in this assumption, middle-class values were actually "northern" middle-class values, and the presumption was that the effort to bring southern society more in line with them would create pressure for change so intense that even the South's calcified social and political structure would be unable to withstand it.

Arguing that economic progress went hand-in-hand with social advancement, observers urged state and local development organizations to sponsor the reforms necessary to bring living conditions, educational opportunities, political practices, and public facilities and institutions in the South up to par with those elsewhere in the nation. A major problem for many small towns and their outlying areas was their physical appearance. Ramshackle buildings, unpaved streets, sidewalks, and roads, and the generally neglected appearance of many residential areas, both urban and rural, had long made the South seem to outsiders every bit as backward and savage as Erskine Caldwell, H. L. Mencken, and other critics had described it. State and local development leaders feared that industrialists would be repelled by examples of neglect and indifference and would presume that such conditions would be present only in a community whose workers were shiftless and whose leaders were unreliable. Development experts condemned speed traps and other examples of corrupt government and law enforcement as deterrents to industrial growth. Union City, Tennessee, leaders learned that their assurances of minimal taxation had scared away at least one investor, who was already appalled that the city's recreational facilities consisted of a "picture show and pool rooms" and that the community had no swimming pool, parks, or municipal golf course. Executives linked the low level of local taxation to a lack of civic spirit, which they also saw manifested in the city's downtown slum and the reputedly poor quality of local schools.

The examples of Union City and other communities that lost new plants to more attractive, better governed towns were often used to prod local officials to lead their constituents in soul-searching appraisals of their community's pluses and minuses. Throughout the South, state development agencies as well as the industrial development divisions of banks, railroads, and utilities sponsored self-study and self-help programs. The Georgia Power Company joined with the Georgia Municipal Association and the Georgia Institute of Technology's Engineering Experiment Station to sponsor the "Certified City" Program. This project helped communities measure themselves against criteria that included general appearance, fire protection, education, planning, and the quality of recreational facilities, in order to make the changes and improvements necessary to win certification as "a superior location for industry and business." Under a similar program between 1960 and 1964, Mississippi towns improved their libraries and sewage treatment plants and launched various beautification projects, all in the name of industrial progress.

When representatives of Chance-Vought Aircraft Corporation announced that they would not move to Dallas unless runways at the local airport were extended by 2,000 feet, the City Council blinked not at all as it approved a Chamber of Commerce recommendation calling for an appropriation of $256,000 to get the job done. In other cities boosters supported such innovations as liquor by the drink as evidence that a town was "progressive." Many local development leaders insisted that public auditoriums demonstrated a community's appreciation of "culture." Others urged citizens to impress their patriotism on visiting industrialists by displaying American flags at their homes and businesses.

The "spruce up in the interest of growth" spirit occasionally got out of hand. Development leaders in Lawrenceburg, Tennessee, orchestrated a campaign for a new hospital and auditorium only to find that executives of a large electronics firm were disappointed that the city had no golf course. Fearing that the plant might be built elsewhere, boosters collected over $60,000 and called in local farmers to grade a nine-hole course. Two months later the course was finished, but the plant was already slated for a Georgia location. Still, Lawrenceburg made its new golf course the focal point of its promotional effort. Elsewhere, when one southern town appeared to lose a plant because it had only a nine-hole golf course, local development leaders did not rest until nine more holes were added. When the town quickly landed a new plant, envious industry-seekers in competing towns fell over themselves in their efforts to equip their communities with golf courses.

Although the improvements supported by development groups often dealt with superficial matters, the desire for more rapid and beneficial economic growth sometimes contributed to movements for political reform. Several 1946 "GI Revolts" saw returning veterans taking active roles in efforts to unseat entrenched political machines. In Hot Springs, Arkansas, veterans followed the lead of Sid McMath, who subsequently made a name for himself as the state's growth-conscious governor. In Augusta, Georgia, ex-servicemen joined business and professional leaders in ousting the "Cracker Party," a local machine whose leadership had produced little more than economic stagnation. The reformers swept into office promising honest, efficient government and more attention to industrial growth, and they quickly staged a community improvement conference at which topics ranged from sewer construction to spiritual education. In New Orleans, DeLesseps S. Morrison successfully linked the corruption of the incumbent Maestri administration to the disappointing pace of economic growth, and rode into the mayor's office on a tide of support from veterans and businessmen.

Convinced that industrialists were impressed by modernized, sophisticated, businesslike government, spokesmen for development groups supported a number of modifications of their state's or community's political structures. In 1930 the Citizens Charter Association, a group of Dallas entrepreneurs, helped push through a plan for city manager government. Civic and business leaders in Atlanta were proud of their reputation for enlightenment and sophistication, but in the post-World War II period they became increasingly concerned that the Georgia capital and the other major cities in Georgia were suffering at the hands of the reactionary, antiurban political tendencies emanating from the state's rural areas. A major source of their frustration was the "county unit" electoral system which assigned not fewer than two nor more than six unit votes to each county. Such a system meant that three tiny rural counties had as much influence on the election of state officials as did the much more populous Atlanta/Fulton County area. Rustic politicians like Eugene Talmadge, who boasted that he had never campaigned in a county with a street car in it, had exploited their popularity in rural areas by practicing their colorful but often irrelevant brand of politics. Development theorists repeatedly warned that such an unprogressive political structure was damaging to Georgia's industry-seeking efforts. Atlanta-area boosters were particularly concerned because they feared that industrialists might shy away from a location where their operations and the lifestyles of their employees might be influenced by the actions of voters in Roberta, Wrens, or Hahira. As a result, Atlanta business and civic leaders supported a court suit that resulted in the final overthrow of the county unit system in 1962 and paved the way for a victory by moderate Carl E. Sanders over free-wheeling former governor Marvin Griffin in the 1962 gubernatorial race.

No state in Dixie suffered from a worse record for political corruption and instability than Louisiana, which had been unable to escape the stigma of wasteful government and hostility to business and industry that had arisen during the Huey Long era. Despite repeated promises from state officials that industry could be assured of a warm welcome, the state's economy lagged behind its regional neighbors, and many industrialists who shunned Louisiana made it a point to stress their concerns about politics, government, and public schools. The development-oriented Public Affairs Research Council examined almost every facet of public policymaking in Louisiana and revealed practices such as the consistent failure of members of the state's revenue department to pay income taxes or the tendency of certain governors to "forgive" the unpaid taxes of their major campaign contributors. The group's spokesmen lobbied for expansion of vocational education and even encouraged members of the state legislature to conduct their proceedings in a more decorous fashion.

The thrust of political reforms sponsored in the name of industrial development was to bring policymaking and governmental practices in line with what was perceived as the businessman's or industrialist's point of view. When development spokesmen supported expansion of public services, they favored the extension of those services that seemed most likely to contribute to economic growth. Otherwise, however, although they opposed reactionary demagoguery, spokesmen for industrial development also encouraged fiscal conservatism and rejected arguments for increased spending for social welfare and other programs geared to the needs of the disadvantaged. The commitment to reform as a stimulus to growth was tempered by a commitment to the low taxes and restrained government also thought to be crucial to industrial expansion.

In the urban South the reforms that accompanied industrial growth and the ones designed to accelerate it reflected a white middle-class orientation. Slum clearance projects made some parts of southern cities more attractive, but they also displaced large numbers of poor blacks. New, low-cost housing units were often inadequate to absorb the displaced, who crowded into the remaining low-income neighborhoods, greatly increasing the likelihood that these areas would degenerate into slums. Clearance programs often left zones of open space that served as barriers to racial interaction. Policymakers generally embraced reforms likely to promote growth and please middle-class sensibilities, but their enthusiasm for programs aimed at needy blacks was more restrained. In Richmond, for example, city officials utilized federal funds in support of a highway project that dislodged 10 percent of the city's blacks, but rejected federal money earmarked for improvement of low-income housing.

The ambivalence with which businessmen and spokesmen for industrial growth approached the crusade to upgrade southern public schools reflected the limitations of the development-inspired reform impulse. The quality of education in the South had been of little consequence so long as the targets of most promotional efforts were industries that required little in the way of mental performance from their employees. As support grew for efforts to attract faster-growing, better-paying plants, however, the need for improved schools became obvious. Sophisticated firms employing upper-middle-class executives and skilled technicians could ill afford to locate where children of their employees could not be assured of adequate preparation for college. The need for better schools therefore became a favorite topic at development symposia across the South, as speakers cited case after case of industries lost because of deficiencies in a community's schools.

In the years between 1940 and 1968, per pupil expenditures in Dixie rose from 50 to 78 percent of the national average. After a point, however, development spokesmen could do little more than express concern for educational reform without compromising their commitment to the low taxes which they also deemed vital to their plant recruitment efforts. With only five southern states spending more than 80 percent of the national norm per pupil at the end of the 1960s, it would be a long time before industrialists could assume that relocating employees would be satisfied with the region's schools.

One area of public education where developers were willing and able to sponsor remarkable progress was that of vocational training. Few economists or promoters doubted that the South's inability to attract better-paying firms was related to its relatively unskilled labor force. Better-trained workers would be able to get better jobs, contended the proponents of expanded vocational education. Florida was a case in point. The Sunshine State had attracted more than its share of engineers and technicians and was well prepared to welcome the aerospace industry in the 1960s. Many of these skilled personnel were in-migrants, but there seemed to be no reason why native southerners could not be trained in the intricate tasks required by the better-paying, faster-growing industries of the future.

Local communities had often taken responsibility for training workers for a new plant, but the kinds of skills which were needed to attract more sophisticated firms could be effectively taught only with expert instruction and the most modern facilities. Publicly supported training programs seemed the most logical means of upgrading the quality of the southern labor force. Such programs would relieve incoming firms of the expense of costly on-the-job-training by providing ready-made work forces theoretically capable of achieving full production levels shortly after a new plant opened. The desire to attract better-paying industry contributed to an expansion of industrial arts and vocational education in most secondary schools, but the labor requirements of many incoming plants were specialized enough to require some post-secondary training. Thus the 1960s saw a rapid expansion of advanced vocational classes, both in junior colleges and in special "vo-tech" schools. Most states set their sights on having one of these training centers within reasonable driving distance of every citizen.

Vo-tech curricula often reflected the skill requirements of established employers and the anticipated needs of new industries likely to locate in the area. Supporters argued that such an approach would help to stop out-migration by holding out to young adults the prospect of attractive employment in or near their hometowns or rural communities. On the other hand, incoming employers would be pleased to find a surplus of workers eager to make use of their newly acquired skills. A neglected consideration was the likelihood that an abundance of skilled workers would shield new employers from pressure to pay top wages in order to attract and retain qualified workers. Thus the new training program might have a less dramatic impact on local wages than its sponsors had promised.

Proponents of expanding vocational education as a means of improving the quality of southern industrial growth were pleased with the proliferation of vo-tech schools, but many of them insisted that a more flexible system was needed in order to respond more rapidly to the specific needs of an incoming plant. Suggestions for such a program first took root in South Carolina, where a legislative study committee recommended a system of "special schools" administered by experts who would plan the curriculum and determine the equipment needs as well as recruit the trainees for the new program.

The start-up program allowed promoters to assure industrialists that a new plant in South Carolina could open with a well-trained work force at or near full productive proficiency, regardless of how specialized the new plant's labor needs might be. "Start Up in the Black" became the motto of the Palmetto State program, and industrialists were soon singing its praises so loudly that other states quickly adopted similar plans. When an industrialist chose a location, he informed development officials of his personnel needs. Start-up staffers then chose a convenient training center, usually a vo-tech school near the plant site, and recruited and instructed the trainees, who received neither pay nor assurance of employment. Hiring decisions rested with the company, and state officials tried to attract more trainees than would be hired, apparently allowing for attrition but also creating an ample supply of qualified workers. Most start-up plans operated in this fashion except for minor variations. Alabama, for example, maintained a fleet of mobile classrooms ready to be placed at the actual plant site if necessary. Most states were prepared to supply instructors or, if not, agreed to pay company employees to conduct the training. The incoming industry invested nothing in the program except the consultative services of its personnel department.

Insofar as it represented an attempt to recruit better-paying, faster-growing industry by creating a ready-made, well-trained work force for new plants, start-up training seemed a significant departure from the New South development tradition. In reality, however, such assistance was simply another form of subsidy, one that appealed to more complex industries by alleviating worries about labor productivity and thereby encouraging more skill-intensive operations to take advantage of the labor, tax, and general cost-of-operating and living advantages that a southern location could offer. The new plant's work force came at taxpayer expense with practically no strings attached, and although most plants utilizing state-trained workers paid wages higher than the regional average, others proved willing to preserve the local labor situation by keeping their pay scales near community norms. Thus, although start-up programs aided in the creation of better-paying jobs, such programs provided no immediate threat to regional wage differentials or the South's reputation as a haven for low-wage industry.

Start-up training was an attempt to upgrade and modernize the South's industrial base, but many of the region's leading proponents of economic growth feared that such programs were still not sufficient to assure the South its rightful share of future development. Research was to be the keynote of the space age, as American industry sought ways to streamline its operations through innovation and technological advances. It was difficult for many to see that such a future had much meaning for the South, whose deficiencies in research skills and institutions were well known and whose past contributions to American technology had been relatively meager. At the end of World War II research scientists were more than five times more numerous in the nation as a whole than in the South, and patents were issued to southerners at a rate less than one-third of the national average. If the South was to gain true economic parity with the nation at large, it had to provide industry with what one observer called "a suitable climate for invention, discovery and innovation."

One of the pioneers in the effort to bring research-oriented firms to the South was Luther Hodges, who as governor of North Carolina devoted a major portion of his energies to the state's industrial development. In the late 1950s Hodges launched a plan designed to capitalize on the research potential of the Raleigh-Durham-Chapel Hill area, where three major universities (Duke, North Carolina, and North Carolina State) were clustered within fifteen miles of each other. Hodges expanded on a suggestion by famed sociologist Howard Odum by proposing the establishment of an industrial research park within the triangle formed by the three universities. Hodges's background as a highly successful textile executive came in handy as he sought funding for the multimillion-dollar project, and he utilized the prestige and expertise of both administrators and faculty of the three schools to persuade various manufacturers of the benefits of locating a facility in Research Triangle Park. Still, the park might never have achieved significant status had Hodges himself not resigned his post as secretary of commerce in 1963 to become chairman of the Research Triangle Foundation. The former governor used all his connections to land an International Business Machines facility for the Triangle, a development that seemed to accelerate the park's growth dramatically. In fact, the research center's management was soon turning away firms that seemed too manufacturing-oriented. By the end of the 1970s twenty-eight research operations were located in the park, working on projects ranging from artificial turf to a synthetic membrane for heart transplant patients. The Triangle had also attracted a number of federal agency offices, including the National Center for Health Statistics and the major research center of the Environmental Protection Agency. Park promoters even succeeded in persuading the American Academy of Arts and Sciences that the Research Triangle was a better site for the Academy's National Humanities Center than Washington, Boston, or Philadelphia. By the mid-1970s the Raleigh-Durham-Chapel Hill area sported more Ph.D.s per capita than any metropolitan area in the nation.

The Research Triangle Park was the South's most successful industrial research center, but all of the southern states committed the resources of their colleges and universities to the cause of industrial development. Across the South, research and development centers held out the prospect of state assistance to industry in solving scientific and technological problems. Like start-up training, public support for research-related industrial growth represented a more sophisticated form of subsidy wherein the state helped to underwrite the costs of experimentation and discovery, thereby contributing to higher profits for the company and more and better jobs for the state's workers.

Beautification, improvements in facilities and services, and greater emphasis on vocational education and industrial research all helped to remove the taint of backwardness that had long marked the South. The major blemish on the region's image, however, remained the intolerance and inequities which characterized its racial relations. The socioeconomic repression of black southerners seemed wholly inconsistent with the progressive, affluent society spokesmen for industrial development promised to build in the South. Yet, prior to the 1950s, those who worked to attract new industry to their region simply followed the lead of Henry Grady by assuring skeptical investors that the South's racial problems had been solved and that southern blacks labored contentedly under the paternalistic supervision of their white friends. Most industrialists accepted the racial status quo in the South, tailoring their hiring, promoting, and paying policies to the caste system and making little or no effort to further the cause of racial equality. As the civil rights concerns of the post-World War II period focused increasingly critical attention on the South's racial practices, however, many political and economic leaders revealed their fears that industrialists might be reluctant to open new plants in a region where the prospect of future controversy loomed so large.

Even before the initial shock from the 1954 Supreme Court desegregation decision had worn off, industrialists expressed concern about asking executives to move their families into states where lawmakers were seriously discussing closing the public schools. As Virginia Governor J. Lindsay Almond, Jr., spewed the rhetoric of massive resistance, Lorin A. Thompson warned that "An increasing number of the new industries in Virginia are having difficulties in bringing into their plants the highly trained personnel needed to guide production and distribution programs. Some skilled workers in these new plants and industries have already left because they regarded the education of their children to be of paramount importance. . . . Any environment which is unstable and in which public education is threatened is not conducive to business development or expansion." Sensing that the integration crusade might also have significant economic impact, angry segregationists charged that efforts to mix the races in the South went hand-in-hand with a desire to undermine the region's development effort.

The Montgomery, Alabama, bus boycott of 1955 caused immediate consternation among the city's businessmen, who were already concerned about their city's difficulties in attracting new industrial investment. Montgomery had apparently lost a DuPont facility and four other plants to other cities in 1954 and 1955. A concerned group of forty businessmen—mainly merchants, realtors, land developers, bankers, insurance agents, and contractors—formed the "Men of Montgomery," adopted the motto "We Mean Business," and launched a crusade to persuade the City Commission to build a new terminal at the airport so that visitors would receive a favorable "first impression" of the city. The crisis over segregation on the buses quickly demanded their attention, however, as negotiations stalled and a bomb exploded on the front porch of the home of Dr. Martin Luther King, Jr.

The recalcitrance of the City Commission frustrated the Men of Montgomery's effort to mediate, and the determination of several prominent lawyers to have black activists prosecuted under the state's 1921 anti-boycott law threatened to make Montgomery a veritable laughingstock. Although the "Men" endeavored to make a compromise seating policy proposal more attractive to blacks by securing a "no retaliation" pledge from the City Commission, boycott leaders rejected the proposal and the next day eighty-nine blacks were indicted for violating the anti-boycott law. The failure of the Men of Montgomery to keep the boycott dispute out of the courts (and thus the headlines) should not obscure the fact that as early as 1956 many of the city's business leaders made a connection between a community's race relations image and its prospects for economic growth, and took action, however limited, to forestall further confrontation and violence.

The first opportunity to assess the economic implications of the integration controversy came in Little Rock, Arkansas, in 1957. Governor Orval Faubus's surprising decision to resist desegregation not only triggered an ugly black-white, state-federal confrontation, but left Little Rock development spokesmen facing the task of convincing potential investors that angry rhetoric, closed schools, and the potential for lawlessness and physical violence should not alter their perceptions of Little Rock as a prime location for a new plant. The difficulties encountered by local boosters as they tried to woo new industry encouraged them to push for an end to the crisis, but their actions apparently came too late to save the city from the economic repercussions of the confrontation. Industrial investment not only created far fewer jobs statewide in 1958 than in the previous year, but Little Rock failed to attract a single new plant from 1958 through 1961.

The "lesson of Little Rock" seemed to be that diehard resistance to desegregation was economic suicide, and groups supporting or willing to accept integration sponsored speaking appearances by Little Rock boosters, who told their city's tale of woe and urged business and civic leaders to do everything in their power to keep their schools open and the local populace calm. Feeling that the policy of massive resistance to desegregation might be undermined if it could be shown to be bad for business, officials of the liberal Southern Regional Council launched the "Southern Leadership Project" in order to persuade businessmen to work for a speedy and nonviolent end to segregation and discrimination in their cities.

The Anti-Defamation League of the B'nai B'rith took a similar approach in *The High Cost of Conflict*, a pamphlet which quoted businessmen from across the South who believed that violence and school closings were disastrous for local economies. The only businessman who claimed the integration crisis had been helpful to him was a Little Rock mover who admitted: "We are moving families away from Little Rock faster than ever before."

The actual impact of such efforts was difficult to assess, but at both the state and the local level southern business leaders and other proponents of industrial growth often played crucial roles in engineering peaceful transitions to token desegregation. On the other hand, in cases where development leaders were slow to involve themselves in the local integration crisis, desegregation was seldom speedy or smooth. In Virginia, pressure from development-oriented business groups apparently encouraged a dramatic turnaround by

Governor J. Lindsay Almond, Jr., who in six months went from vowing to close the public schools to urging the Virginia legislature to scrap a statewide school closing law in favor of a local option plan that allowed individual communities to make independent decisions about whether their schools would remain open in the event of an integration threat.

Georgia followed a similar pattern after the legislature appointed an investigative committee chaired by influential Atlanta banker John A. Sibley. A majority of the Sibley committee apparently ignored the sentiments of a majority of white Georgians by recommending a local option plan instead of statewide school closings in the event of desegregation. The influential Atlanta business and civic community believed their city had a significant stake in the state's desegregation crisis. Longtime Mayor William B. Hartsfield had painstakingly forged a reputation for moderation exemplified by his insistence that his was a city "too busy to hate." As early as 1955, Hartsfield had engineered peaceful desegregation of the city's golf courses, and as a final showdown neared over school desegregation he drew on the support of prominent businessmen and boosters and the influence of the Atlanta *Journal* and *Constitution*, whose editors insisted that the state's economic future hung in the balance in the desegregation crisis. As the Georgia capital faced an integration showdown in the fall of 1961, reporters flocked into Atlanta, ready to chronicle the ugliness and violence that had accompanied integration in other southern cities. They received a healthy dose of hospitality from Hartsfield and other local officials, and when the well-orchestrated token desegregation left them little to report, the mayor provided the scribes with a bus tour of the city.

Atlanta was not the only southern city to follow such a moderate course. Businessmen and development leaders became the advance agents of peaceful desegregation in both Dallas and Charlotte. By the same token, the integration crises in New Orleans, Birmingham, and Oxford suggested that violence and distasteful publicity were more likely when the response of influential economic leaders was belated or half-hearted. Although self-styled progressive Mayor DeLesseps S. Morrison promised to avoid mob rule in New Orleans, representatives of the Chamber of Commerce and other development leaders remained silent as court-ordered school desegregation neared. Morrison warned that lawlessness could undermine efforts to bring new industries to the Crescent City, but receiving no public support from local boosters he reportedly declared, "If those S.O.B.'s aren't going to do anything, I'll be damned if I'm going to stick my neck out." The result of Morrison's and the business community's reticence was weeks of ugly confrontations wherein young black pupils were cursed and taunted by local white mothers. It finally became apparent that such adverse publicity could be translated into dollars and cents when the city's tourist trade fell off precipitously, and the crisis wound down only after local business and professional leaders followed the lead of groups like SOS ("Save Our Schools") by signing a widely publicized statement calling for a return to law and order.

In neighboring Mississippi, as the state's best-known university faced its integration showdown in 1962, industrialists and promoters remained silent while bellicose segregationist Governor Ross Barnett vowed defiance. Even after the violence which erupted upon James Meredith's arrival in Oxford, leading manufacturers and businessmen found it difficult to formulate a meaningful call for moderation. Reports of industrialists cancelling plans to locate in Mississippi were front-page news across the nation, and a *New York Times* account even claimed that one factory had been moved across the state line into Louisiana in order to avoid a Mississippi mailing address.

Birmingham's business and professional leaders also seemed oblivious to potential damage to the city's economy as they stood by silently while local political leaders sacrificed parks, playgrounds, professional baseball, and performances by various musical and theatrical groups, all in the name of Jim Crow. The United States Steel Corporation had long dominated the local economy, and its executives had little interest in recruiting new industries that might compete with them for labor and thereby bid up wages. Moreover, the steel company's executives took the position that they should not become involved in the affairs of the local community. With its corporate and professional leaders standing silently by, Birmingham drifted from one image-spoiling episode to another. The failure of police to protect the "Freedom Riders" in 1961 was an example, as were the seventeen bombings of black churches and homes between 1957 and 1962. The city plunged into even deeper controversy in the spring of 1963 as civil rights demonstrations gave segregationist City Commissioner Eugene "Bull" Connor the excuse to retaliate with police dogs and firehoses. Only after the demonstrations became particularly intense did fifty white businessmen representing the "Big Mules," the city's legendary economic elite, meet with local and federal officials and black leaders.

In the fall of 1963 the bombing deaths of four black children in Birmingham and the furor surrounding Governor George C. Wallace's insistence on personally blocking integration at the University of Alabama apparently caused a number of industrial prospects to announce that they had dropped Alabama sites from consideration. Wallace's segregationist stand was a matter of concern to many Alabama industrial developers despite the fact that the governor was a tireless crusader for new industry who insisted that his position on separation of the races was no impediment to his recruiting activities. Wallace did receive significant support for his segregationist stand from businessmen and boosters within and without Alabama, but many executives were obviously nervous about meeting with the governor, apparently fearing adverse publicity.

The Hammermill Paper Company found itself at the center of a storm of controversy after it announced its decision in early 1965 to locate at racially troubled Selma, Alabama. Clergymen, black activists, and students all threatened a boycott of Hammermill products. Executives claimed to have made their decision before Selma law enforcement officials engaged in some of the most blatant abuse of demonstrators that was to occur during the entire civil rights movement, but the company severely tarnished its image by the move, nonetheless.

Unlike George Wallace, other governors who won reputations as "go-getters" where industrial development was concerned were usually associated with moderation on racial issues. This was clearly the case with Leroy Collins of Florida and Luther Hodges of North Carolina. When tokenism superseded massive resistance as the preferable response to integration demands, segregationists such as Ernest Hollings and Donald Russell in South Carolina began to place more emphasis on jobs and payrolls than on maintaining "the southern way of life." Moderate Carl Sanders won the Georgia governorship in 1962 over former governor Marvin Griffin, whose questionable ethics and continued adherence to segregation had little appeal in the state's urban areas.

The desire for industry was on occasion a potent force for moderation during the civil rights era, but a state's attractiveness to industry may have had little relation to the manner in which its desegregation was handled. Arkansas and Mississippi showed considerable percentage growth in manufacturing employment between 1960 and 1967 despite their racial troubles, but neither state was the beneficiary of a large increase in the absolute number of jobs created during the period. On the other hand, while Texas, North Carolina, and Tennessee, states with more "moderate" reputations, led the region in absolute gains after 1960, these states had also outdistanced their neighbors in the preceding decade. In sum, the "lesson of Little Rock" notwithstanding, it was difficult to establish statistically that either ostentatious moderation or well-publicized resistance to desegregation had any impact whatsoever on a state's industrial growth.

The expectation that industrialists would demand racial equality in any area they chose as a plant location ignored the fact that prior to the activism and federal pressure of the 1960s few industries appeared to have any difficulty accommodating themselves to racial conditions in the South. Industrial executives probably expressed concern about racial problems in a prospective location largely because the prevailing national climate of opinion seemed to demand it. As protests and media coverage focused critical attention on certain communities, executives like those at Hammermill discovered that choosing such a controversial site for a new plant might subject their company to heavy criticism or even consumer boycotts. It was not so much the actual progress that an area had made in race relations as its ability to avoid public controversy that may have been a factor in some plant location decisions. A 1962 survey revealed that the "moderation" of southern business leaders extended to opposition to violence but little further. A poll of Tennessee manufacturers found only 4 of 308 expressing any concern whatsoever with a community's progress in race relations as they chose among prospective locations. Having dealt with a number of industrialists seeking sites in the South, Arkansas superbooster Winthrop Rockefeller cynically observed: "The industrial prospect doesn't give a hoot whether your schools are segregated or not, but he wants no part of disorder and violence."

The largely superficial concern of incoming industrialists with race relations allowed development-minded political leaders to play a skillful game of tokenism. After a race riot in June 1967, Tampa's Chamber of Commerce was instrumental in obtaining a $60,000 matching grant to create a program of advanced academic and on-the-job training for Tampa youths. Despite pledges of support, the city's businessmen failed to contribute even one-third the amount needed to keep the program going.

Although Atlanta's influential businessmen played an important role in token integration of schools as well as civic and professional organizations, the city's economic leaders also took steps to insure that downtown urban renewal property would be used for commercial development rather than public housing for blacks and other low-income groups. Across the South there was little evidence that promotional leaders followed up their calls for moderation with further efforts to promote racial harmony once the initial threat of adverse publicity was gone.

If the influential economic leaders who became the reluctant advocates of moderation were not deserving of praise for their social concern, they nonetheless merited recognition for the service they grudgingly performed. The significance of taking the "first step" in the confrontation atmosphere of the civil rights era South should not be minimized. As late as 1964 when the Jackson Chamber of Commerce issued a timid, grudging call for compliance with the newly passed Civil Rights Act, the Mississippi House of Representatives went immediately into special session to censure the Chamber. The lawmakers declared: "This deplorable act of calling for slavish obedience is a contravention of everything the State of Mississippi has fought for and stands for . . . it constitutes aid and comfort to the integrationist, communist, and socialist minorities of the nation." Still, the fact that Jackson's business and industrial leaders were willing to brave such a reaction indicated that even in the South's most race-obsessed state, the pursuit of industrial/economic progress had pulled alongside the preservation of white supremacy as a matter of concern among influential political and economic figures.

Liberal Mississippi journalist Hodding Carter observed that his paper encountered more criticism when it raised questions about industrial development than when it advocated integration. Carter might have received a different reaction had the two issues been juxtaposed, but support for industrialization was nonetheless strong enough to provide an anchor for the South's racial moderates. In the tension-packed atmosphere of the early stages of the civil rights movement, even the decisionmakers who realized the futility of resistance needed a rationale for softening their stands. For many political leaders at both the local and the state level the goal of more jobs and a better standard of living was the only excuse for retreat which they could expect most of their constituents to accept. The moderation espoused by the South's industry-seekers may have been hollow, hypocritical, and self-serving, but it kept a number of cities from reenacting the ugly scenes of New Orleans, Oxford, and Birmingham. Had majority opinion held sway, these scenes and worse might have been commonplace across a South whose white populace seemed to support defiance at any cost up to and including school closings and violence. Thanks to the efforts of many advocates of moderation from the business and industrial communities, the decision to resist or acquiesce was taken out of the hands of the majority. The raving and ranting may have continued thereafter, but within a state once a single community's schools or a single state university had experienced token integration, the back of massive resistance was effectively broken.

The desire for new and better industry brought a number of significant reforms and innovations to the post-World War II South. Beautification, expansion and improvement of hospitals, parks, and other public facilities clearly contributed to an improved quality of life for many Dixie residents. Political reform helped to modernize and streamline policymaking and to rid southern politics of some of its more primitive characteristics. Yet concern for the expectations of industrialists did little to induce a greater degree of social consciousness among the region's decisionmakers. Rather, the emphasis was on fiscal responsibility and the extension of only those services that might earn a relatively direct dividend in terms of economic development. As for incoming industrialists, they appeared to be interested in reform primarily as a means of improving overall efficiency and providing the most favorable operating environments possible. The quest for more rapid and economically beneficial industrial growth had its greatest educational impact in the area of vocational training, where it stimulated the proliferation of area vocational centers and spawned quick-response "start-up" programs that provided new plants with work forces made ready at state expense. Calls for improved industrial growth also pushed more public resources in the direction of research support for incoming firms. Like "vo-tech" programs, expanded research and development efforts amounted to another form of public assistance wherein the state invested in a company's efforts to develop the new processes and products necessary to maintain or expand its work force. Thus, as in the case of a bond-financed, tax-exempt plant, there was still significant pressure for public officials to cooperate with management by insuring that unwanted pressures and demands did not materialize. Wage scales improved after the advent of expanded training and research programs, but most incoming employers continued to tailor their pay scales to local norms, and those who did not often hired too few workers to have any but a localized impact.

The desire for improved industrial growth had its most significant social impact in the area of race relations. Efforts by economic development leaders to avoid violence and distasteful confrontations produced only a small, token step toward equality, but this step was at least a beginning on which consistent federal pressure might build.

The southern economy underwent significant modernization after World War II, as did the region's racial customs, politics, and public institutions and facilities. Yet a careful analysis demonstrates that the social, political, and institutional changes accompanying industrialization were far less extensive than those anticipated by the social theorists who expected industrial development to transform the South. These experts had blamed persistent conservative, rural, agrarian traditions for the backwardness of southern society, but they were at a loss to explain why an urbanized, industrialized South failed to become the classic liberal capitalist society once envisioned as the inevitable product of southern industrial growth.

Many of those who saw economic progress as the agent of social progress in the South believed that economic expansion would enlarge and energize the region's middle class. The desire of this new bourgeoisie for an accelerated rate of growth and an improved quality of life would presumably lead them to adjust policies, practices, and institutions to the fundamentally middle-class values of mainstream American society. Stability was one of the highest priorities of the middle class, and in most modern industrial nations pressures from an organized, upwardly mobile working class had posed enough of a threat to stability to force the bourgeoisie to support reforms aimed at creating and maintaining a more open, egalitarian society. Despite the South's industrial growth, however, resistance to unionization and the enduring chasm between black and white workers freed middle-class leadership from significant pressure to take southern society beyond where they wanted it to go. Civil rights protests did force grudging tokenism from state and local officials, but these activities owed much of their effectiveness to external pressures, both from the government and from the corporate decisionmakers whose ostensible aversion to racially troubled states and communities was well publicized, if exaggerated. Once the protests were quieted and the state's and community's good name assured, leaders of the South's business and commercial classes could return their attention to the reforms needed to foster an environment conducive to efficient business and industrial operation and compatible with the values and lifestyles of an expanding middle class. These reforms aimed at gradual improvements in education, health, transportation, and other public facilities, but they hardly threatened a redistribution of wealth or influence. In short, they constituted an agenda for change but not for sweeping change, and certainly not for the transformation of southern society as a whole.

The civil rights movement culminated more than half a century of growing pressure on the South's leaders to take steps against the racism, repression, anti-intellectualism, and institutional backwardness that had earned the South its benighted reputation. The grudging progress in race relations and the economic strides of the 1960s relieved some of this pressure, as did the Republican party's "southern strategy" and the successive trauma of white backlash, Vietnam, and Watergate which toppled American self-righteousness from its lofty, self-assigned perch. A new, less judgmental spirit permeated the national temperament, making many Americans more appreciative of the South's progress and more tolerant of its lingering deficiencies.

The newly respectable Sunbelt South found itself under less pressure to change than at almost any time during the twentieth century. The post-World War II South had experienced relatively significant changes in race relations, government, politics, and public services and facilities, but changes in conditions and attitudes, north as well as south of the Mason-Dixon line, had also helped to shorten the region's journey toward national acceptance. As the South moved closer to the American mainstream, the mainstream also shifted in the direction of the South.

6. Natural and Environmental Resources and Industrial Development

The coal company came
with the world's largest shovel,
And they tortured the timber
and stripped all the land.
Well, they dug for their coal
'til the land was forsaken,
Then they wrote it all down as the progress
    of man.[1]

John Prine's description of the fate of his father's hometown at the hands of stripminers was intended to muster public outrage against further destruction of the Appalachian environment. Yet the conflict between conservation and environmental protection on the one hand and the desire to stimulate the South's economy and provide jobs for its impoverished masses on the other was seldom the clear-cut, good-versus-evil struggle that Prine depicted.

For most of the post-Reconstruction century industrialists and promoters of economic development assumed that the South's natural resources were there for the taking. Cheap, abundant raw materials were a keystone of the New South appeal, and the concepts of conservation and environmental protection were too esoteric to stand

---

[1] "Paradise" by John Prine. © 1971 by Walden Music, Inc., and Sour Grapes Music.

up against the region's seemingly insatiable desire for more industrial payrolls. Rivers, trees, the soil, all could be taken for granted—jobs were the truly precious commodity in an economically deprived Dixie.

It was only in the more environmentally sensitive atmosphere of the 1970s that southern policymakers encountered significant pressure to protect the region's physical environment from further damage. Political and economic leaders faced a dual and often perplexing challenge—that of continuing to promote industrial expansion while protecting the environment from the potentially damaging effects of that expansion. With so much of the region's recent economic progress attributable to the attraction and retention of relatively affluent resident consumers, the problem of protecting the environment while facilitating future growth came to symbolize the dilemma confronting political and economic leaders of the Sunbelt South. How could the relatively unspoiled and uncongested living conditions so clearly related to recent economic growth be reconciled with the reputation for cooperative, minimally restrictive government that seemed fundamental to the South's attractive business climate?

New South development policies offered the region's raw materials and natural resources to investors with practically no questions asked. Next to labor, timber, minerals, and abundant water were the major advantages that spokesmen for industrial development emphasized in their sales pitches to northern investors. The South's natural resources seemed limitless, and in an age when environmental consciousness was all but nonexistent there was little reason to view a butchered forest or an eroded hillside as much of a sacrifice, especially if the benefits of industrial jobs for large numbers of economically deprived southerners were considered. Unrestrained access to raw materials and natural resources thus became an implicit element of the favorable business climate which promoters held out to new industry.

A striking example of the late nineteenth-century South's insensitivity to the environmental impact of industrial development came in the southeastern corner of Tennessee, in Polk County's Great Copper Basin, where copper mining began in the mid-nineteenth century. After a pre-Civil War boom resulted in the removal of most of the rich surface ores, would-be miners quickly discovered that lower-quality ore could not be profitably shipped out of the mountainous area. Further mining made sense only if this cruder copper ore could be reduced to a purer and more valuable product before it left the basin. The answer to this dilemma was "roasting" the ore for several days on smoldering piles of cordwood in order to burn the heavy and worthless impurities away from the copper.

Roasting was the key to continued mining in an area where the returns from agriculture or lumbering were generally meager. It not only helped to keep local residents employed at the mines, it created a sizable demand for wood, so much so that by 1900 roast heaps were consuming 1,000 cords per month. The surrounding countryside quickly took on a butchered appearance both because of the rapid cutting and because of a crucial side-effect of the roasting process. Burning copper ore produced large amounts of sulfur dioxide, a foul-smelling gas which was not only irritating to the nose and eyes but often damaging to trees and deadly for smaller vegetation. By 1900 a fifty-square-mile area around the mines had become a raw, red desert as barren as a moonscape. Each rainfall produced more erosion and filled nearby streams with mud, while heavy downpours often flooded low-lying areas. On humid, rainy days with a low cloud ceiling, a sulfur dioxide fog or mist settled down on the surrounding countryside, killing or stunting crops, gardens, and trees.

Farmers and timbermen in both Tennessee and nearby Georgia howled their complaints but usually to no avail. Local judges hesitated to antagonize companies that dispensed a half-million-dollar payroll in an otherwise deprived area, and the dispute came to a head only after frustrated Georgians, tired of rebuffs from the Tennessee courts, turned to their own government for relief. Realizing that the mines employed many Georgians, state officials were reluctant to act, but they finally yielded to pressure from North Georgia lumbermen and farmers and filed suit against the Tennessee companies in the United States Supreme Court. After several years of legal wrangling and other delays, the court issued an order in 1906 requiring the companies to pursue a suggestion by Georgia attorneys that the sulfur dioxide could be captured and converted into sulphuric acid for use in making fertilizer. If these efforts failed to alleviate the smoke damage, Georgia's attorneys might return to the court for a permanent injunction against further smelting by the companies.

Even Justice Oliver Wendell Holmes's opinion in favor of the state conveyed the hope that Georgia would not take action to shut down the mines and throw hundreds of men out of work. The companies echoed this theme repeatedly, and even after continued complaints by local farmers and timbermen whose livelihoods were threatened by the sulfur dioxide's effects, state officials declined to request a final injunction, settling instead for an agreement whereby the companies would theoretically release no sulfur dioxide whatsoever during the growing season, and during other periods would file regular reports of their smelting activities with the Georgia attorney general's office.

Hope that this agreement would end the controversy was short-lived. Angry farmers and timbermen claimed the companies frequently violated their pledge to restrict their emissions during the growing season, and expert observers warned of the permanent effects of the acid mists which would gradually destroy remaining soil fertility, convert marginal farmlands into wastelands, kill timber, and damage the area's road systems by encouraging erosion. Finally, in an effort to quiet the continuing protests, the state of Georgia renegotiated its agreement with the largest of the copper companies, agreeing to the creation of a board of arbitration which would assess damage claims and make cash awards, if justified. With the company paying the arbitrators, the results were predictably unsatisfactory for local farmers and timbermen, but state officials refused to entertain suggestions that the arbitration system was flawed, and disillusioned north Georgians soon decided it was not worth the effort to file a claim.

The companies continued their harmful emissions unchecked by any constraint other than the carelessly administered agreement until the early 1970s. The Tennessee Copper Company's ostentatious efforts to reclaim the ruined land enjoyed only limited success as the red earth rejected even the kudzu plant. The Copper Basin ultimately became less well known for its mineral output than for its desert-like appearance. The long controversy illustrated the problem which southern leaders faced as they sought to expand their region's economic base at the expense of the natural resources that provided the livelihood of nonindustrially employed southerners. Even without the damage caused by the sulfur dioxide the area would not have produced high-quality timber or supported profitable agriculture. On the other hand, copper company payrolls were large and workers in the mines and smelters drew wages much higher than the average for either state. Shutting down or drastically reducing the operations of the copper companies would have had severe economic consequences for many local residents. While a present-day perspective suggests that no adequate price tag may be attached to environmental purity, those who were attempting to resolve this dispute saw their mission as one of preserving the greatest immediate tangible economic benefits for the most people.

In cases where residents of the New South were expected to choose between conservation and economic gain, the latter almost always won out. Coal mining began in western Kentucky in the 1820s and spread to the eastern counties over the next two decades. In the last quarter of the nineteenth century investors who recognized the importance of coal swooped down on the Kentucky hills. More often than not buyers for the coal companies purchased not the land itself but only the coal it contained, thereby avoiding tax obligations during the period before railroad construction cleared the way for mining coal deposits. In return for the mineral wealth of land capable of yielding up to 20,000 tons of coal per acre, the owner received from fifty cents to five dollars per acre. Subsequent court rulings decreed that when an unsuspecting mountaineer signed away the mineral rights to his land, he surrendered not only all the coal, oil, and natural gas beneath the surface, but the timber rights (mine shafts needed supports) as well. Moreover, the coal companies had purchased the right to use the surface of the earth in any way necessary to remove the coal, including road construction and the diversion of streams. Finally, the companies were not obliged to avoid water pollution or any other environmental damage their activities might produce.

Future generations would discover that the willingness of the courts to honor ancient and obviously unfair contracts left them powerless to use or preserve the land they ostensibly owned. According to Harry Caudill's account, as a judge dismissed a mountaineer's suit against a coal company for ruining his water and destroying his cropland, he expressed his sympathy but noted that under current appeals court rulings "about the only rights you have on your land is to breathe on it and pay the taxes. For all practical purposes the company that owns the minerals in your land owns all the other rights pertaining to it."

After the mid-twentieth century such literal interpretation of these old contracts proved particularly damaging to areas that had already received more than their share of environmental abuse from subsurface mining. Even the most efficient operations had not been able to tap the rich but narrow "outcrop" seams near the surface which, as a practical matter, could not be mined from within. As earth-moving technology improved, companies turned increasingly to "stripmining", employing dynamite, bulldozers, power shovels, and dump trucks to gouge out the rich coal that was inaccessible from inside the ground. Stripmining required relatively few workers and such an operation could often extract a ton of coal at half the cost involved in removing a similar amount from deep in the earth.

The true cost of stripmining fell on local residents and landowners. In flat areas the bulldozers scraped away the topsoil and covered it with subsoil clay, giving the surface of the land an ugly and infertile bricklike texture that was easily eroded into nearby streams. In the mountains the environmental damage produced by stripmining was even more devastating. Trees and topsoil tumbled down the hillsides, followed by the mud and rubble displaced by the mining. Waste coal, often high in sulphur content, was left exposed to rainfall, which caused it to bleed sulphuric acid into creeks, often killing everything attempting to live in the streams. Naturally, heavy rains and snows confronted valley dwellers with the threat of floods or avalanches caused by displaced rubble. Cooperative legislatures and jurists seldom made trouble for stripminers, as in the case of Morehead, Kentucky, where even the public roads were condemned in order to facilitate the operations of the Peabody Coal Company.

Miners faced tougher restrictions in the 1970s, but a great deal of damage, some of it irreparable, had already been done. The traditional reluctance of state and local officials to "burden" mine owners with regulations had left two million acres (an area roughly the size of Rhode Island and Delaware combined) in Appalachia covered with coal mine waste. Until 1964 Kentucky law required the filling of old mines "only where practical." Many mining operations had simply ripped out as much subsurface coal as possible and left nothing but wooden timbers to support the roof of the mine, the result being dramatic, often dangerous shifts in the earth's surface. A *Wall Street Journal* writer described the appearance of a village in a mined-out portion of Appalachia: "The streams around this crossroads hamlet run yellow-red with acid drainage from mines. Huge, bare strip mine excavations slash across the miles of once green mountains. Vacant mine buildings rot and sag. Dusty abandoned mining machinery clogs rutted back roads." Efforts to facilitate the mining of Appalachian coal not only brought environmental and ecological ruin but many stripmine areas became virtual ghost towns where those who chose not to flee faced unemployment rates up to 30 percent.

The South's timberland often suffered a fate similar to that of its coal country. In the 1880s northern investors turned increasingly toward southern forests, particularly Mississippi's, where full-grown virgin softwood stood in huge quantities. Mississippi forests were much closer to American and foreign markets than those of the Pacific Northwest, and the mild climate and moderate terrain made cutting simpler and less arduous. Thus it was understandable that speculators invested heavily in Mississippi timberland, which they purchased at almost nominal cost. For example, a single Michigan buyer acquired nearly three-quarters of a million acres of prime longleaf pine. Seeing the trees as little more than annoying obstacles to cultivation, unthinking farmers were usually ready to sell the timber on their lands for whatever they could get.

Agrarian interests, fearful of the influence of the foreign corporations that owned the timberlands, helped to maintain tax policies that timber owners assailed as unfair. Relatively heavy annual taxes on standing timber and the reluctance of assessors to reevaluate partially cut timber holdings encouraged lumber companies to cut as rapidly and as thoroughly as possible. There were other incentives for rapid deforestation, including the fact that standing timber was often used as mortgage collateral and usually had to be converted to cash as rapidly as possible. Because so much of the virgin timber had achieved full maturity, delays in cutting promised no benefits from growth but definite risks from rot or insects. The cutting therefore proceeded at breakneck pace, with axes and saws stripping away all the marketable timber while "skidders," in dragging the fallen trees, uprooted seedlings and left the "cut-over" land devoid of any but secondary vegetation. Tax laws did nothing to encourage reforestation, which seemed an economically foolish undertaking so long as significant virgin timber remained. Efforts to convert the butchered forest lands were half-hearted and the results pitiful. Unwilling or unable to wait for reforestation to pay off, many landowners forfeited their formerly lush timberlands to the state rather than continue to pay taxes on them.

The experience of lumber towns where companies had stripped the forests of all marketable timber with no thought for reforestation demonstrated the degree to which a decision to sacrifice environmental resources to short-term economic goals could have a disastrous long-term economic effect. The Gulf Lumber Company, which "clear cut" the area around Fullerton, Louisiana, found no takers in 1927 when it advertised: "Pretty and prosperous city worth $3,500,000 priced at $50,000; Fullerton Mill will close soon for all time. Homes for workmen will be razed unless someone finds new industry that would pay there." Years later the area had been reforested but no trace of Fullerton remained except a mill pond and a few crumbling foundations.

The Upper Texas Gulf Coast area had its share of pollution problems even before oil was discovered. Houston and other cities were plagued by the thick smoke spewed out by coal-burning trains. Lumbering had laid some areas bare to the ravages of erosion, and cotton farming had worn out the soil in others. Urban sewage disposal compounded the pollution damage. Still, the impact of this pollution was all but negligible compared to the damage accompanying the oil boom that began early in the twentieth century. In this era the gusher became a symbol of prosperity, so much so that promoters deliberately sent thousands of gallons of oil shooting into the air in order to encourage potential investors to sink their dollars into new wells. The damage and waste resulting from such showmanship was of little concern. In the scramble to outdistance the competition, conservation and efficiency were trampled underfoot. Overflows soaked the surface of the ground while rapid pumping drew salt water into the local water systems. Wooden tanks and earthen pits leaked profusely and the path from pump to tanker was marked by frequent spills.

Many plants distilled off only the more valuable products—kerosene and gasoline—and dumped the remaining crude. Some refineries burned crude oil to fire their distilleries, releasing large amounts of acrid smoke which combined with the sulphur fumes and hydrocarbons to create a major air pollution problem. Houses in Beaumont were periodically discolored by the acrid fog blanketing the area.

As the examples of the Copper Basin, the Kentucky coal fields, the Mississippi and Louisiana timberlands, and the Texas Gulf Coast suggest, prior to the late 1960s few if any southern leaders gave any thought to the long-term environmental implications of industrial development. With local communities prepared to offer free buildings, tax exemptions, and numerous other favors, it was not likely that a southbound plant's executives would encounter any questions about their plans for waste disposal or odor control. James Fallows cited an agreement whereby Savannah, Georgia, boosters even promised to protect the Union Camp Paper Company from any legal action that might result from the plant's polluting activities: "It is agreed that in case litigation arises or suits are brought against you on account of odors and/or flowage from the proposed plant that the Industrial Committee of Savannah will pay all expenses of defending such suits up to a total amount of $5,000."

Such cooperativeness may have been essential to bringing a new plant into Savannah, but subsequent generations would pay the price for the license to pollute given Union Camp in the 1930s. By 1969, 80 percent of the industrial contamination in Savannah could be traced to Union Camp. Many of the wastes the company poured into the Savannah River consumed oxygen as they decomposed, thus making it difficult for plant and animal life to survive in the river. Union Camp was not solely to blame for ruining the Savannah. An American Cyanamide plant dumped large amounts of sulfuric acid wastes into the stream, a Continental Can plant added its discharges, and the city of Savannah used the river to dispose of its raw sewage. The few fish that survived this deadly barrage were unfit to eat, and some observers claimed that the water was acidic enough to sear human skin. The Savannah also absorbed heavy industrial wastes 160 miles upstream at Augusta. The Augusta-based Olin Corporation's mercury waste leaks became so dangerous that in the summer of 1970 fishing was prohibited anywhere in the stream between Augusta and Savannah.

Just as industries that dominated local economies faced few

challenges to their wage and labor policies, such plants were often free to damage the environment with impunity. Paper companies were the South's most conspicuous polluters, probably because the odors they emitted were not only pungent but detectable over great distances. Other industries drawn to the South by the region's natural resources were also often responsible for pollution. Chemical producers found the southern locations attractive because the region offered an abundance of water. Unfortunately, disposal of liquid wastes from such plants was often a problem. Storage ponds could easily spring leaks, especially in wet weather, and a single wrong turn of a valve could ruin nearby lakes and waterways. With various plants dumping mercury and bauxite wastes into the stream, scientists discovered sixty-six chemicals in portions of the Mississippi River which provided New Orleans with its water supply. Observers linked reports of these discoveries to the inordinately high rate of cancer in the state. Industrial wastes apparently drove the brown pelican from the Louisiana Gulf Coast. Oil spills by coastal petroleum operations were always a threat, and every new drilling operation destroyed more coastal oyster beds.

Prior to the late 1960s southern leaders often proved willing to bend, break, or ignore pollution-control statutes that threatened to impede industrial development. When new laws were written, major industrialists often managed to persuade legislators to tone them down by requiring that protecting the environment be reconciled with maintaining growth and employment.

Despite a history of insensitivity to environmental problems, the southern states were nonetheless caught up in the wave of public concern about pollution that manifested itself at the end of the 1960s. As pollution control became a top federal priority, conservative, states' rights-oriented legislators pushed for tougher statutes, often as a means of heading off increased federal regulation and involvement in their states' affairs. State after state toughened pollution laws, increasing fines for violations and subjecting future industrial growth to closer scrutiny by environmental protection officials. One Kentucky court set aside Friday afternoons for citizens to appear with any and all complaints against local polluters. Even state development agency spokesmen acknowledged the environmental fervor, pledging to recruit no industries that were obvious polluters and promising to involve their colleagues in state pollution-control agencies in their negotiations with prospective investors.

Despite the official hard line toward potentially polluting industries, in their actual dealings with executives, political and economic leaders managed to convey the clear impression that they were still significantly more concerned about economic growth than about environmental protection. Many plant seekers refused to accept the idea that there was any such thing as a "bad" or undesirable industry. Even in a decade of greater regulation and "choosiness," some local governments apparently still did their best to overlook industrial pollution. The Justice Department charged in 1972 that Memphis officials had allowed the Whitaker Corporation to dump untreated copper, zinc, and chlorine wastes into the Mississippi River. In 1977 the Monsanto Corporation faced charges of releasing dangerous chemicals into the Coosa River in Alabama. In Hopewell, Virginia, an Allied Chemical plant was cited for allowing potentially dangerous amounts of poisonous kepone to seep into the local water supply.

Efforts to clean up and preserve the environment collided head-on with the traditional open arms attitude toward any and all industry that had brought so many potentially polluting facilities to the South. As Samuel Walker noted, the South's economic backwardness gave it "greater incentive" to court the nuclear industry. Southern states led the way in calling for state-level responsibility for nuclear regulation, though spokesmen generally displayed greater interest in promotion than in safety. The region's hospitality to the nuclear industry reaped significant economic benefits. By the early 1960s the payroll at the Atomic Energy Commission's Oak Ridge, Tennessee, facility totalled nearly $122 million annually, while the payroll at the Savannah River Nuclear Plant added more than $50 million more. AEC purchases in the South in 1962 pumped approximately $39 million more into the region's economy. In the same year 24 percent of the commission's more than 200,000 employees worked in the South. At the end of the 1970s public concern about the safety of nuclear power plants, heightened by the near-disaster at Three-Mile Island, Pennsylvania, focused attention on the nuclear plants which had been so warmly welcomed in many of the southern states.

No state in Dixie had more avidly pursued the nuclear industry than South Carolina, which by 1979 got nearly 50 percent of its electric power from nuclear sources. Several accidents and errors at one of the state's nuclear power plants combined with the concerns raised by the Three-Mile Island scare and the almost simultaneous appearance of the movie *The China Syndrome* caused some South Carolinians to suggest that state officials might have been too hasty in rolling out the red carpet for any nuclear firm that came their way. Horror stories of near "accidents" at TVA nuclear power plants also contributed to public concern, but many southerners expressed little doubt about the safety of nuclear facilities, choosing instead to accept at face value the assurances of utility officials that such operations promised more jobs and a better standard of living and were far more of a blessing than a threat.

In areas with little industry, environmental protection clearly took a back seat to the need for more payrolls. In South Carolina, the case of Georgetown's downtown steel mill demonstrated the difficulty of protecting the environment in a locality with a large unemployed population. The Georgetown Steel Corporation, a German firm, located its operation within the coastal city over the protests of many residents, most of whom complained about the heavy dust that was soon covering downtown homes and buildings. On the other hand, the area's large, economically depressed black population preferred working for a polluting industry to cutting wood for a living. The state's development officials had rolled out the red carpet in order to lure the plant to Georgetown, arranging for the construction of docking facilities and pressuring the Corps of Engineers to build a channel between the plant and Georgetown harbor. Environmentalists lamented the widely publicized accounts of the damage caused by the steel plant, but businessmen and black leaders were willing to overlook these problems because of the $10 million payroll that Georgetown Steel dispensed annually.

An even more complex dispute arose near Georgetown at Hilton Head Island in 1969 when the Badisch Analin and Soda Fabrik Company (BASF) announced plans to build a petrochemical plant in Beaufort County, South Carolina. Like Georgetown, the Beaufort area was economically depressed, and state development officials had jumped at the opportunity to land the BASF facility. The state offered the company an attractive package of highway dock construction and tax exemptions, but the developers of the plush resort community on nearby Hilton Head quickly raised a howl, claiming that the BASF plant would be environmentally damaging and would destroy the area's appeal to tourists. Supporters of the project offered evidence of the economic benefits the plant would bring, and local residents prepared a "welcome" petition. As in Georgetown, black leaders argued that economic concerns should take precedence over environmental ones. NAACP representatives noted that if the area remained under the domination of the resort industry, blacks could look forward to no better future than manicuring golf greens or cooking and cleaning for wealthy white tourists.

When BASF finally scrapped its plans to build in the area, many environmentalists celebrated what they hailed as a great victory with but little thought as to whose victory it was. The resort's promoters publicly expressed their pleasure that the area's beauty had been preserved. They failed to mention, however, that their resistance to the BASF plant had also preserved a surplus of cheap black labor to perform the menial, low-paying tasks at the island's hotels, restaurants, and other facilities. If indeed the BASF affair produced a victory for the environment, it offered local blacks little hope for a more economically secure future.

Marshall Frady quoted the director of a local job placement service, who saw the BASF controversy in these terms: "When it comes to a choice between the people I know who have to make it here on food stamps, who're still living like they've been living for the past hundred years, or whether we're gonna keep all these pure water ways and beautiful marshes and wildlife, all this wonderful scenery—I got to go with the people. If I got to put the oyster beds up against people, the oyster beds have to go."

As the federal government's role in environmental protection expanded, southern development leaders hoped that their efforts to bring new plants into relatively unindustrialized areas would not be affected. Their hopes rested on the fact that such areas had far cleaner air and water than federal statutes required. Southern leaders felt it reasonable to assume that rural counties might continue to absorb new industries so long as environmental conditions did not deteriorate below national guidelines. In 1972, however, the Supreme Court's verdict in the *Sierra Club* v. *Ruckelshaus* case shattered this illusion by affirming a lower court decision that the Clean Air Act of 1970 was intended to prevent any decline in air quality, even in areas where pollution levels fell far below federal maximums.

Southern development leaders feared a "no-growth" future when Congress began in 1976 to debate several amendments to the Clean Air Act which would not only prohibit significant deterioration of air quality in "clean air" areas, but would also put strict limits on the emissions of new facilities constructed near national parks or unprotected streams. Southern senators joined with their western colleagues to oppose these amendments, arguing that states and localities should be allowed to determine their own growth rates. A number of political and economic leaders complained that the proposed policies would virtually halt industrialization in their areas. Some southern leaders injected sectionalism into the debate, suggesting that the amendments were part of a conspiracy to halt Dixie's growth. Southern senators attempted unsuccessfully to delete the "no significant deterioration" provisions from the amendments, which were blocked entirely in 1976 by filibustering Senators Jake Garn and Orrin Hatch of Utah, a state with plenty of clean air but comparatively few industries. Southern and western senators joined forces against the amendments again in 1977, but this time the stricter regulations passed despite their efforts.

The apparent insensitivity of many southern political and economic leaders to environmental damage stemmed from the fact that every state had its pockets of poverty and unemployment. It was one thing to talk about protecting the quality of the air in Birmingham or Atlanta, but quite another to fret about pollution in Camp Hill or Vidalia. As worthy as it was, the goal of environmental protection simply took a back seat to creating enough jobs to improve the standard of living in underdeveloped areas and to stem the out-migration which drew young adults away from these localities. Many who opposed stringent environmental regulations did so because they feared that in too jealously guarding natural resources they might forfeit the long-sought opportunity to develop their area's human resources.

Environmental protection was one of the few "causes" that appeared to maintain its vitality throughout the 1970s. Thus, when a southern leader suggested that pristine air or water was less important to his state or area than jobs and payrolls, he invited the scorn of environmentalists and liberal journalists alike. In reality, however, while it was not necessarily true that a clean environment was incompatible with industrial development, in cases where choices had to be made it was by no means certain that a majority of the residents of any area would reject a new plant simply because it would make the air smokier or some of the water unfit to drink. Environmental purity was an eminently supportable principle in the abstract, but there was little evidence that most southerners or other Americans were at any time willing to support it at the sacrifice of an opportunity for personal or community economic progress. A 1971 poll showed South Carolinians overwhelmingly in favor of both stringent regulation of industrial emissions and continued efforts to attract heavy manufacturing and chemical plants. If South Carolinians deserved to be criticized for failing to see the contradictory nature of their responses, they were surely no more guilty in this respect than representatives of the Industrial North, who hoped that the "no significant deterioration" provisions of the 1977 Clean Air Act Amendments would discourage industry from moving out of areas where pollution levels remained well above federal maximums.

Since the New South era, southern industry-seekers had used the region's business climate as a major selling point, promising that industries could look forward to hassle-free operation with minimal interference from governments that were more interested in protecting industry than in regulating it. Yet by the 1970s the freedoms promised to industries came into conflict with the prospect of gracious, uncomplicated lifestyles that had proven so attractive to the Sunbelt South's affluent in-migrants. The more like Youngstown or Newark the South became, the less likely it was to attract disgruntled former residents of such areas. On the other hand, the greater the efforts to prevent the South from becoming an environmental carbon copy of the Northeast, the less attractive it became to industrial investors. One of the many paradoxical difficulties accompanying continued industrial development was the threat to the South's physical appeal posed by the very economic growth that appeal had helped to stimulate.

7. Why the New South Never Became the North: A Summary

Industrialization has brought many changes to the South, but skyscrapers, smokestacks, and industrial parks have not destroyed the region's cultural distinctiveness, nor have they provided solutions to many of the problems traditionally associated with its historically underdeveloped economy. In fact, industrial development has not only failed to establish general prosperity but has left a large number of southerners mired in poverty.

Despite a widespread perception of the Sunbelt South as a newly prosperous paradise, in terms of absolute statistics rather than growth momentum the South of the 1980s remained the nation's number one economic problem. In 1980 only Texas had a per capita income above the national average, and the South was still home to more than 44 percent of the nation's poverty population. More than a quarter of Mississippi's population lived below the poverty level, and Virginia was the only southern state with a poverty percentage below the national average.

Impressive percentage improvements in per capita income notwithstanding, constant-dollar figures revealed that between 1960 and 1980 Mississippi and Kentucky fell more than $200 further below the national average, while Arkansas, the Carolinas, and Georgia also lost ground. Cheap nonunion labor continued to be the South's major attraction to industry, and industry seekers still took great pains to inform employers of their community's abundance of eager workers. In February 1976, for example, the Rock Hill, South Carolina, Chamber of Commerce proudly circulated statistics showing that nearly three-quarters of a 25,000 person sample of the local labor force still earned less than $5,000 per year.

Emphasis on cheap labor undermined efforts to recruit better-paying industries that would not only bid up wages but enhance the prospects for unionizing southern workers. Employers who had been lured to the South by pledges of protection from unions often forced local chambers of commerce and other booster organizations to turn a cold shoulder to firms that might infect the community with unions and/or higher wages. Employers in the textile belt were particularly hostile to such companies, and several cities lost large, high-paying plants because of the resistance of local industrialists.

There was little doubt that the South's nonunion climate helped to depress wages. In 1980 North Carolina was the region's most industrialized state. The Tarheel work force was also the nation's least unionized (less than 7 percent) and its workers the most poorly paid (74 percent of the national hourly wage). North Carolina's well-publicized industrial "progress" notwithstanding, average hourly manufacturing wages fell from $1.05 below the national average to $1.90 below it between 1972 and 1980.

The self-satisfaction of the Sunbelt South's boosters ignored the numerous economic disparities within the region. Some areas owed their Sunbelt prosperity to the "most favored colony" status that allowed them to receive the spinoff benefits from northern industrial progress and eventually put them in a position to attract new residents and investments when the Industrial North began to decline. On the other hand, other areas seemed to have little hope of ever transcending their quasi-colonial status, and still others lost even that. "Progress" had played a cruel joke on Appalachia, which, as much as any area in the South, met Immanuel Wallerstein's criteria for a "peripheral" region because it supplied the northern "core" states with vital but "lower ranking goods . . . whose labor is less well rewarded."

According to Ronald D. Eller, Appalachia's experience with what was supposed to be progress has actually left it "a rich land with poor people." As mountaineers became timbermen, miners, or millhands, a healthy barter economy centered around the family farm gave way to a colonial system that operated for the benefit of absentee employers and entrepreneurs whose businesses drew the mountaineer's wages out of the hills. A relatively open, informal society gave way to a more rigid social and political hierarchy presided over by the mill and mine owners. "Suspended halfway between the old and the new," Eller writes, "the mountaineers had lost the independence and self determination of their ancestors, without becoming full participants in the benefits of the modern world." When their resources were depleted, many parts of Appalachia were simply left for dead without hope for economic, environmental, or cultural resurrection.

In the Deep South, areas with impoverished, unskilled black populations also found it difficult to attract new industries of any sort. In such areas marginal farmers and agricultural laborers struggled to survive on a few hundred dollars a year but never appeared in unemployment statistics. A 1973 study of four rural counties revealed the effects of a persistent labor surplus. Scarcely 42 percent of potential workers were actually participating in the labor force. Black heads of households averaged only $3,403 a year in earnings, a figure well below half the national average. Nearly 25 percent of all male household heads worked more than 49 hours per week (as compared to the national norm of 10 percent). The wages earned by rural workers were so low that more than one-third of all sub-poverty level families were supported by someone employed full-time. Education and skill levels remained so low that there was little hope of attracting better-paying industries to any of these counties. Despite significant overall economic progress, in 1980 more than 35 percent of all southern blacks still lived in poverty.

While many areas dominated by low-wage industries failed to share in the Sunbelt boom, other communities which had industrialized during the decades before and immediately after World War II became miniaturized versions of declining Frostbelt cities. The economic problems of the late 1970s and early 1980s severely injured the nation's heavy industries, and many southern towns reeled from the impact of the losses in manufacturing or manufacturing-related operations. Fayetteville, Tennessee, leaders bemoaned a long list of industrial and commercial closings that even shut down the city's "Dairy Queen" ice cream parlor. Meanwhile, as businesses collapsed or contracted, Fayetteville's abundant industrial park space failed to impress potential investors. Such towns might actually have benefited, at least temporarily, from out-migration, but instead many of them continued to absorb significant population growth. The Corinth, Mississippi, area saw its population expand at a rate of 21.5 percent during the 1970s, while the unemployment rate climbed as high as 15 percent by early 1981.

In the meantime, areas which had never attracted a significant amount of industry experienced heavy out-migration as residents fled to the region's cities, drawn by the hope of opportunities which often did not exist—at least for them. These new urbanites often found greater income disparities among city dwellers than they had encountered in rural areas. A large number of these migrants were black. In Georgia, the urban black population grew by 37 percent between 1970 and 1980. For many of them the aura of prosperity surrounding the South's larger cities was little more than a glittery veneer. For example, Mayor William B. Hartsfield's effort to blend racial moderation with headlong pursuit of growth had made Atlanta a regional model. The city's ultra-busy airport became a gateway to the South, and its downtown area dwarfed its regional counterparts with a skyline of high-rise hotels replete with their own lakes (doubling as cocktail lounges) and well-nigh stratospheric revolving restaurants from which tourists and conventioneers could simultaneously survey both Atlanta's history and its future. The underside of the Georgia capital's success story was less attractive. As blacks moved in, whites moved out, leaving the city with a two-thirds black population by 1980. Few blacks went into the high-rise hotels or other showplaces unless it was to clean them or provide services for a steady stream of conventioneers. Atlanta's ghetto was by no means the nation's worst, but as the "homicide capital" of the Deep South, the city became as well known for its broad daylight slayings as for its downtown glitter.

By 1980, Houston, the city most often depicted as the brightest spot in the Sunbelt, also had an array of problems easily as troubling as its growth was encouraging. Houstonians were two-thirds more homicidal than New Yorkers but the city's population explosion left an understaffed police force (one officer per 600 residents) struggling to provide anything approaching decent protection. Traffic jams in Houston were predictably horrendous with 200 new automobile registrations a day in a city of nearly 2 million where only about 10 percent of the population rode the buses regularly.

Fast-growing Florida attracted a family of four every six minutes. Not only did this runaway growth threaten to deplete the underground water supply, it also left urban areas with major air and water pollution problems. One journalist predicted Florida was "going to die of thirst or choke to death on a glut of people, exhaust fumes, concrete and sewage."

In addition to maldistribution of income and simultaneous urban sprawl and decay, the South's leaders confronted the challenge of making the region's industrial/economic growth pay off in terms of improvements in the quality of life for all southerners. Much of the hoopla surrounding the Sunbelt phenomena had suggested that the South offered a more attractive living environment than the Industrial North. When statistical evidence was considered, however, it became apparent that the region had a long way to go before it measured up to the rest of the nation in terms of public services, equal opportunity, and overall levels of living. A major problem lay with deficiencies in institutions and services directly supported by taxation. Promises of minimal or in some cases no taxation had long been an important element in the South's appeal to new industry, but reluctance to increase taxes seemed to deny state and local governments the resources needed to cope not only with the demands created by economic growth but with the needs of those whom that growth had not touched. A 1977 analysis by the Southern Regional Education Board indicated that state and local governments in Dixie were utilizing only about 79 percent of their taxing capacity as compared to a national average of over 95 percent. The mainstay of the revenue system was the sales tax, which took a proportionately larger bite out of the incomes of the South's much greater than average share of the nation's poor. Mississippi, for example, utilized more than 160 percent of its estimated sales taxing capacity. Meanwhile, the effective business tax rate in the southern states was less than 60 percent of the nonsouthern average.

Mississippi's struggle to improve its public schools demonstrated the degree to which the traditional approach to economic progress in the South may have actually stood in the way of both human and economic progress. Mississippi's reputation as the nation's most educationally inferior state rested on the absence of even a mandatory attendance law, let alone public kindergartens. To fund a program of compulsory education with kindergartens, Governor William Winter suggested in 1981 that the legislature increase the state severance tax on oil and natural gas. Winter argued that by providing better education for its youth, Mississippi would enhance its prospects for economic growth. Not so, contended his opponents, who warned that low taxes were crucial to the state's continued economic progress, and who cited a 1980 business climate study that placed Mississippi in the number one position. When a watered-down version of Winter's program finally passed in 1982, its funding came from a modest increase in the state's income tax rate and a one-half percent increase in the already overworked sales tax, but the severance tax remained unchanged.

As the leaders of Mississippi and other southern states continued to exhibit a desperate hunger for more growth, some thoughtful writers and scholars began to question whether industrialization had been worth the cost. In the exciting first years of the Sunbelt boom many southerners had found it difficult to contain their pride in their region's economic accomplishments. Songwriter Bobby Braddock had used the traditionally uncritical medium of country music to celebrate the South's ascendance:

I see wooded parks and big skyscrapers
Where once stood red clay hills and cottonfields.
I see sons and daughters of sharecroppers
Drinking scotch and making business deals.[1]

By equating progress with the opportunity for young southerners to behave like Yankee capitalists, Braddock's song raised the question of whether the South had been striving all these years for nothing more than to be like the North. For some observers the growth of the 1960s and 1970s resurrected the old concerns best expressed by the Nashville Agrarians that an economic transformation would destroy the most positive aspects of the "southern way of life."

---

[1] "I Believe the South Is Gonna Rise Again" by Bobby Braddock. © 1973 by Tree Publishing Co., Inc. International copyright secured.

Writing in 1973 concerning the "Americanization of Dixie," John Egerton worried that "the South and the nation are not exchanging strengths as much as they are exchanging sins, more often than not, they are sharing and spreading the worst in each other, while the best languishes and withers."

Fearing that rapid growth raised the threat of a "cultural lobotomy," Marshall Frady bemoaned the fact that "for the last few decades the South has been mightily laboring to mutate itself into a tinfoil-twinkly simulation of southern California, and in the process has unwittingly worked on itself a spiritual impoverishment. Faulkner's Flem Snopes has evolved into a relentlessly bouncy and glitter-eyed neo-Babbit with an almost touching lust for new chemical plants, glassy-maized office parks and instant subdivisions. The mischief is that, in its transfiguration into What-a-Burger drive-ins and apartment wastelands, the South is being etherized, subtly rendered pastless, memoryless and vague of identity."

The biting accuracy of Frady's descriptions and the note of concern he sounded quickly call to mind the unheeded warnings of the Agrarians, whose critique of industrialism became more meaningful in an era when the undesirable side effects of industrial growth had finally become a reality. Ironically, many of those who were once the impoverished South's sternest critics now saw in its rags-to-riches story much to lament. They appeared to have finally discovered that, just as the Agrarians had insisted, the backward South of yesteryear had possessed some redeeming qualities after all. Much of its distinctiveness had been the result of seemingly primitive attitudes and customs, but the late 1960s and 1970s had revealed these conditions as national rather than regional characteristics. For all its flaws, the South was at least a place unto itself, and all southerners, black or white, shared in a peculiar regional heritage. To paraphrase Flannery O'Connor, all southerners were at least "from somewhere." John Egerton recalled a black Chicagoan visiting relatives in Tuskegee, Alabama, who explained: "Chicago ain't where I live. It's where I stay. Chicago's *existin'*. Tuskegee is *livin'*." It was a sad paradox that the economic progress once thought necessary to solve the South's problems now threatened many of the human interactions and physical attributes that even at its most deprived, benighted worst, had made it seem a good place to live.

Had the Agrarians been right? Was the South's birthright bartered for a mess of pottage (and thin pottage at that)? The neo-Agrarian observers of the 1970s attacked the negative results of industrialization but, like their conservative predecessors, they provided no relevant alternatives for coping with regional economic problems. Conceding that economic growth had been a mixed blessing, one southern newspaper editor quoted by Joel Garreau nonetheless reminded a visitor, "It beats the hell out of pellagra." As they lamented the urban sprawl of an Atlanta or a Houston and shuddered as the small-town South disappeared under a tidal wave of parking lots, K-Marts, and fast food emporiums, most writers failed to realize that the people who fought over K-Mart's "blue-light specials" and wolfed down pizza and tacos viewed such opportunities as genuine examples of personal and societal progress. Imperfect as it was, the story of Dixie's industrial growth was a success story for a great many southerners, especially those who remembered the futility of tilling worn-out soil and the pain of explaining to their children why the family could not afford a decent place to live or a respectable automobile. If the factory fell far short of paradise, it nonetheless became a refuge for many southerners who felt they had no place else to go.

The South's bittersweet experience with industrialization was not atypical of a developing society. Economic gains often require cultural sacrifices, and nostalgic references to the good old days when times were bad increase in proportion to the pace of economic change. Industrialization had been so earnestly advanced as a panacea by so many scholars, politicians, and business leaders, however, that even the much ballyhooed Sunbelt South was something of a disappointment. Despite recent gains an ascendant South had yet to achieve statistical parity with a declining North, in terms of either income or the quality of public services and institutions. If an Americanized Dixie had to sacrifice some of its southern charm, should it not at least have acquired more of the positive attributes of northern industrial society?

Liberal journalists and social scientists had fervently hoped that industrialization would create in the South the same affluent progressive, egalitarian, socially conscious society they believed it had spawned in the North. The South's ability to industrialize without becoming thoroughly "northernized" points to the need to explore the reasons why the South developed differently, rather than persist in the use of a largely irrelevant "northern" model to study the southern industrial experience.

Students of social change in the South invested so much faith in industrialization because they associated it with the rapid urbanization that accompanied the industrial revolution in Great Britain or the Industrial Northeast. The model of the classic industrial city was most clearly defined by sociologist Louis Wirth. For Wirth, the behavior-modifying potential of the urban environment derived primarily from heterogeneity: "The personal traits, the occupations, the cultural life, and the ideas of the members of an urban community may therefore be expected to range between more widely separated poles than those of rural inhabitants." Wirth's city was a whirlpool of human interaction whose impersonality freed residents from the traditional restraints imposed by small-town life. In the city class and presumably even racial barriers would crumble as competition and interaction destroyed the misconceptions that held people apart.

Wirth's model became gospel to students of the South. As the civil rights movement got underway, urbanization seemed almost synonymous with the demise of segregation. In 1958, for example, sociologists J. Milton Yinger and George E. Simpson asserted that "urbanization, the increase in industrial jobs with hourly pay rates, the beginnings of unionization, diversification of jobs for negroes, the growth in literacy and awareness of democratic values, the sharp increase in the size of the urban middle class, a growing integration of the national economy—these and other forces are changing the patterns of race relations in all parts of the country." Statistics documenting persistent and even expanding segregation did little to discourage scholars like the sociologists who looked in 1971 at an already urbanized South and insisted that "the social structure characteristic of the older feudal and agrarian South is being rapidly dismantled and left behind in response to the demands of urban living."

One of the most important contributions to social progress expected to accompany urbanization was the growth of the urban bourgeoisie. For many experts the South's lack of a viable middle class had long been the key to its social backwardness. The focus on the middle class as an agent of progress rested on the impression that the bourgeoisie in industrial societies had traditionally embraced social activism and reform. Sociologist Leonard Reissman argued that "in our own history, in the history of other western nations and again today in the events in newly emerging nations, the middle class has assumed the pivotal role of promoting social development." Reissman also contended that the middle class forces a "restructuring" of society: "The middle class in a developing area provides the leading personnel for social modernization. It is the social segment most committed to such development, for its future power and prestige depend on it. . . . the driving aspirations of middle class persons push them toward social modernization as the means to realize their ambitions." Finally, the middle class thrives in "an open class society oriented toward achievement" and pulls "the rest of society along with it toward higher living standards, broader educational opportunities, and wider participation in the society."

The middle class became the "missing link" in the South's evolution as a society because of a combination of economic, social, and political factors that kept the region off what Jonathan M. Wiener called "the classic capitalist path that had been blazed by England in the seventeenth and eighteenth centuries and followed by the Northern states." William H. Nicholls identified one of the great "ifs" of southern history when he argued: "Had the pace of the South's post-bellum industrial development actually matched that of the earlier Industrial Revolution of England or New England . . . the Southern middle class would have flowered more profusely on the basis of a rural yeomanry which could have supplied much more good business talent if southern outlets for that talent had been more plentiful."

Wiener, Dwight Billings, Jr., and other Marxist scholars sought to explain the "non-classical" nature of the postbellum South's economic, social, and political development by providing evidence for the impressionistic assertions of Wilbur J. Cash, who had argued that the plantation mentality stood at the center of southern society as late as the eve of World War II. Thus the region's middle class remained subservient to the values of the planter, the result being a process of "conservative modernization" based on a pattern of economic growth that was compatible with the survival of the plantation and beneficial primarily to a small but powerful coalition of planters, merchants, and industrialists.

The conservative modernization model indicated that the problem with the South's middle class in the late nineteenth and early twentieth century was one not only of size but of structure and orientation as well. Although there were significant differences in lifestyles, like their small-town counterparts, many members of the urban middle class were tied to the agricultural and processing activities of the countryside. Profits from the sale of farm products and the extraction and processing of raw materials, as well as from the distribution of these products, depended on low wages, labor control, and minimal taxation. At the same time, the economic health of planters and processors determined their ability to purchase the goods and services provided by the region's merchants and professionals. So long as this economic interdependence persisted, the South's middle class was unlikely to sponsor policies that would upset planters or conservative industrialists. Most merchants, bankers, and lawyers could have ill afforded to join the agrarian insurgents of the 1880s and 1890s had they been seriously invited.

When a reform movement finally came in the form of Progressivism, it naturally reflected the dominant political, economic, and moral concerns of the planters and commercial middle class. Disfranchisement defused the explosive potential of a challenge from below and ostensibly eliminated much of the corruption infecting the electoral process. At the same time, better schools, expanded public health facilities, and prohibition promised healthier, more productive, and controllable workers. Railroad regulation provided more efficient and economical transportation of farm and factory products, as did the heralded "good roads" campaigns. The expanded public services and improvements in municipal governments and facilities that accompanied the Business Progressivism of the 1920s were urban-oriented but they seldom threatened the status quo in the hinterlands. The small-town interests that dominated state legislatures readily accepted the reforms that benefited them and tolerated those that promised no harm.

Not only did the South's distinctive pattern of economic development alter the size and orientation of its middle class, preventing it from fitting the classic capitalist bourgeoisie model applied by social scientists, but the region's pattern of industrial location also made the Wirthian "urban-industrial" model inapplicable. The heavy concentration of industries that were not conducive to rapid urbanization left the majority of southern cities dependent on agricultural commerce, and the urban bourgeoisie still reluctant to challenge the region's political and socioeconomic hierarchy. Because of their labor orientation, by the early twentieth century most southern industries chose rural and small-town locations where they could tap the growing surplus of unskilled, fresh-off-the-farm workers. In 1969 nearly 40 percent of the South's industry was situated in a rural or small-town setting. This dispersed locational pattern reflected the importance of competitive, labor-intensive industry to the region's economy. Firms seeking abundant, cheap, nonunion labor found the rural South teeming with eager workers ready to commute long distances each day. Textile-laden South Carolina typified this pattern, with only 33 percent of its industrial plants located within the corporate limits of a town in 1969.

Scattered about the countryside, small southern manufacturing plants boosted local economies without disrupting the social and political hierarchy evolved by a labor-surplus agricultural society. In addition to the workers, the major beneficiaries of the expansion of such industries were the merchants, bankers, and other professionals who sold goods and services to the local plant's employees. Preferring the "bird in hand" benefits of perpetuating a reasonably favorable economic status quo to the potential gains accompanying higher wages for local workers, the commercial and professional elite embraced the employer and supported his demands for labor control and protection from wage agitation or union harassment. Industrialists usually returned the favor by avoiding competition with local farmers for labor, primarily by refusing to hire blacks and by looking instead to a large pool of deprived whites eager to, in their words, "work for wages," however low they might be.

In the long run a mutuality of interests facilitated the acceptance of rural and small-town industrialists into the "county seat governing class" once dominated by planters, merchants, and professionals and still a largely conservative force in southern politics. Numan Bartley described this group as "profoundly conservative, combining the social values of plantation agriculture with the normal conservatism of successful townsmen. Dependent on cheap labor and surrounded by a sea of poverty, they treasured social stability."

With its fortunes linked inextricably to plantation agriculture and elementary manufacturing, the small-town elite acted as an agent of inertia in southern culture and politics. The antiurban system of political representation that was so common in the South protected rather than stifled the interests of the region's boondocks capitalists, who seldom aspired to more than maintenance of the status quo in race relations, wage scales, taxes, and governmental cooperation and support. Instead of undermining the influence of conservative rural values, much of the South's late nineteenth- and early twentieth-century industrial development not only accommodated itself to but actually capitalized on and perpetuated the existence of these values.

The conservative modernization model assumed that the reconciliation of planter and industrial interests in favor of the planter was responsible for the course of southern economic development. This assumption could be valid only if there were significant differences between the priorities of conservative planters and those of conservative industrialists, and then only if there existed an alternative path to regional development that had been blocked by the planter-industrialist coalition. Recalling Gavin Wright's judgment that the South's economic future had been largely shaped by its failure to develop a strong nonagricultural sector before the end of the cotton boom, and William N. Parker's analysis of the market and resource factors that so restricted southern economic expansion, it is difficult to argue that the South's industrial development could have proceeded much differently, whether the region was dominated by the planter or the businessman. Lacking the large deposits of iron and coal, the skilled workers, and the investment capital available in the North, the South had little to offer industrialists except cheap labor. Repression of labor was as vital to the New South's industrialists as it was to its planters. Harold D. Woodman underscored this reality when he noted: "The desire for a dependent, easily controllable, docile and cheap labor force burns as fiercely in the heart of a thoroughly bourgeois factory owner as it does in the heart of a plantation owner."

Where slavery had once allowed planters to practice "unfettered capitalism," the post-Reconstruction South allowed similar freedom not only to planters but to industrialists as well. The story of the relationship between the two groups appears to have been less one of conflict resolution or coalition building than of an occasionally tense but relatively peaceful coexistence based on the freedom both groups enjoyed to pursue the interests they shared. These interests often conflicted with the long-term economic and human interests of southern society as a whole, but even if freed from the clutches of its conservative leadership, the South might still have been unable to escape the resource and market influences that kept its economy hemmed in for nearly a century after the Civil War.

With both internal and external economic, social, and political conditions favoring continuity over change, the South lumbered into the Depression era with its power structure reflecting the interests of what Ralph McGill described as a "small town rich man," who owned the best house in town and "according to his geographic location, the gin, the turpentine works, the cotton warehouses, the tobacco warehouses. He was a director in the bank." From the town's biggest store he sold seeds, patent medicines, poultry, and livestock remedies. He not only "controlled credit," but he had a pipeline to his senator, congressman, or governor, and helped to select local officeholders and representatives. Being a "pillar" of the church did not deter him from openly cursing Roosevelt and the New Deal, and he was not above inciting the local Klavern or his handpicked sheriff to run labor organizers out of town. Finally, he had little enthusiasm for large, high-paying industries likely to create competition for "his" labor.

McGill felt that the "small town rich man" was "in trouble" as the 1930s began, but the threat to his stereotypical power broker was not as immediate as McGill perceived it. The cumulative effects of boll weevil, Depression, and relief helped to alleviate concerns about a labor shortage and made many such local barons more enthusiastic about industrialization, provided they had to make no sacrifices to promote it. The bonding and tax subsidy programs that emerged in the 1930s were acceptable because they transferred the costs of industrial recruitment to the general public. Meanwhile, a potentially unstable labor surplus (fed by farm mechanization) was reduced to a more manageable size (with the aid of continuing outmigration), while local merchants and professionals enjoyed the benefits of increased spending fueled by new payrolls.

So long as future industrial development could be controlled, there was little reason for the local power structure to oppose it, and actually much reason to favor it. To insure proper control the Agricultural and Industrial Board which oversaw Mississippi's BAWI subsidy program had more than adequate planter representation, but none from organized labor. The early BAWI plants were screened carefully in terms of their vulnerability to unionization and were located outside the Delta. For the most part, only plants that would pay low wages and agree not to hire blacks need apply for a BAWI subsidy.

Across the South the intensified and expanded commitment to industrialization was in large measure a response to the agricultural modifications that resulted from the onslaught of the boll weevil, the Depression, New Deal farm programs, and World War II. The perception that agriculture could no longer sustain the economy and overall stability of the rural and small-town South convinced many merchants, professionals, and financiers that industrialization was an absolute necessity.

By the Depression era the plantation economy had both an industrial and an agricultural component. The events stretching from the boll weevil invasion through the Depression and the New Deal and into World War II reduced the economic as well as the social and political influence of the agricultural component. Yet, while it paved the way for it, the modernization of agriculture did not trigger the immediate, rapid industrial growth necessary for the complete destruction of the plantation system because the new programs, subsidies, and "blank check" promises to industry left the old pattern of dependence on labor-intensive, low-wage industries fundamentally unchanged. Ironically, plantation-style industrial development persisted even as traditional plantation agriculture was fading away.

The changes that resulted from agricultural mechanization and consolidation as well as the desire for further, more rapid industrial growth ultimately produced a division of interests within the South's middle class, but this cleavage emerged slowly. In the short run, just as the agrarian insurgence of the 1880s and 1890s had helped to tighten the bonds among large planters, merchants, and industrialists, the New Deal left conservative black-belt whites and many southern industrialists more united in their opposition to the Democratic party's increasingly liberal orientation on civil rights and labor issues. Their mutual antipathy to the New Deal and to a party that appeared to be turning its back on the South formed the basis for the 1948 Dixiecrat revolt. In many ways the Dixiecrat movement had a more distinctly economic tinge than had the anti-New Deal phenomenon. The campaign involved a number of influential corporate leaders who had no previous record of political participation. A study of forty-three Dixiecrat leaders found twelve lawyers, twelve banking and corporate representatives, one planter, and an official of the National Association of Manufacturers. Dixiecrat vice presidential nominee Fielding Wright was a former corporation lawyer who as governor had been an enthusiastic proponent of Mississippi's BAWI program.

Numan V. Bartley concluded that the "Dixiecrat movement established the basic neobourbon nature of the reaction that was to play a central role in southern politics during the following decade. It fixed the broad aims and many of the programs that were to carry over into massive resistance." Neobourbon values as defined by Bartley were "essentially rural values" but they nonetheless embodied the New South ethos. Neobourbons showed considerable admiration for corporate capitalism, and thus their political philosophies represented "a blend of the less progressive features of farm and factory."

Neobourbons despised progressive taxation of all kinds, preferring the regressive sales tax if taxation was an absolute necessity. Though ardent advocates of laissez faire, they raised no objection to subsidies and other examples of favoritism toward the manufacturer. Predictably rabid in their antiunionism, they were enthusiastic proponents of right-to-work legislation. For the most part, however, they favored improvements in public education, particularly vocational training, as a means of facilitating economic progress. The same was true of highway improvement, although the commitment to both was tempered by a determination that government should remain small and fiscally sound, so sound that significantly higher taxes on income and property would be unnecessary.

In the wake of the 1954 *Brown* v. *Board of Education* decision, neobourbon abhorrence of the prospect of racial equality manifested itself in the Citizens Council, which might be aptly described as a genuine grassroots resistance organization—at the county elite level. The Council's greatest support came from local leaders in black-belt counties. The movement was born in Indianola in the Mississippi Delta, and its charter members were the local business and civic leaders who helped recruit their counterparts in other Delta counties. Despite its black-belt orientation, the Citizen's Council drew significant support from businessmen and industrialists such as the wealthy insurance and foundry executives who helped form the American States Rights Association in Birmingham in 1954. There was also considerable evidence of behind-the-scenes involvement in the Alabama movement by some of the "Big Mules" who made up Birmingham's economic elite.

As they established an ideological basis for massive resistance to school desegregation, the South's conservative political leaders espoused a synthesis of reactionary economic, political, and racial ideology in defense of the status quo in Dixie. The racial issue was paramount, but it was not totally separable from the economics of growth and laissez faire or the politics of sectionalism and neobourbonism, neither of which was separable from the other. Ernest Hollings of South Carolina was not simply rambling when he vowed: "We are not going to have labor unions, the NAACP and New England politicians blemish the Southern way of life."

Although the South's middle class had been associated with certain significant reforms in the first two decades of the twentieth century, its representatives had favored stability over the disequilibrium and loss of status that might accompany any attempt to remedy the fundamental inequities of the region's social, political, and economic system. For the most part the middle class had accepted the questionable techniques that crushed the agrarian movement and had offered little opposition to the resubjugation of blacks in the late nineteenth century. Only in the closed political system afforded by disfranchisement were the modernizing and occasionally humanitarian Progressive and Business Progressive reforms possible, and no group benefited more from improvements in education, health, transportation, and other public services and facilities, as well as increased governmental efficiency, than the region's business and industrial bourgeoisie. This same group welcomed New Deal largesse and the improvements it could bring but grew increasingly restive as administration sympathy toward organized labor and the national Democratic party's growing solicitousness toward blacks seemed to threaten Dixie's socioeconomic hierarchy. The Dixiecrat movement and its heir apparent, the Citizen's Council, represented a reassertion of a desire not just for white supremacy but for the stability and all of the other political and economic advantages it afforded.

The Dixiecrat and Citizens Council movements notwithstanding, steadfast opposition to change proved less viable after World War II, which, coming on the heels of the boll weevil, Depression, and New Deal, introduced the most disruptive influences that southern society had encountered since Reconstruction. The South emerged from the war as a more agriculturally mechanized, industrially modernized, and relatively more urbanized society.

A growing business and professional middle class found the old agriculturally based power structure dominated by the "small town rich man" too narrow, inefficient, and generally antiquated to meet its changing needs. In the post-World War II period a cleavage appeared in the region's middle class between the more plantation-oriented "Old Guard," for whom maintenance of traditional social and political relationships was of primary importance, and a newer group of ambitious economic and political leaders intent on more rapid integration of the South into the nation's commercial and industrial economy. This latter group played a meaningful role in the reform movements of the early postwar years by assailing political primitivism and governmental inefficiency as impediments to economic progress. Although not openly hostile to the Dixiecrats, these new "moderates" avoided the racial demogoguery traditionally associated with conservative southern Democrats.

Repression and stonewalling had been the customary approach to the preservation of racial stability, but many influential white southerners gradually realized that the civil rights issue could not be defused so long as external federal pressure could be exerted on the southern white power structure. The "lesson of Little Rock" was one that economic leaders who were committed to continued expansion felt they could ill afford to ignore. Heightened national awareness of the plight of black southerners created a climate in which image-conscious leaders of large corporations (whose investments in new plants southern boosters so ardently coveted) had little choice but to announce that they wanted no part of cities and towns with a poor race relations reputation. The impact of these pronouncements depended to some degree on the structure and orientation of state and local economies. A flourishing trade center such as Atlanta, rapidly emerging as a prime location for regional and even national corporate headquarters, was more sensitive to industrialists' expressions of a desire for racial peace in potential investment areas than was the state of Mississippi, whose economy was probably the South's least modernized and whose attractiveness to dynamic industries was relatively limited. Thus Atlanta's business community stepped forward to head off rancor and violence in Georgia's integration crisis, while Mississippi's economic elite hung back until lives—and a great deal of respect—had been lost.

Federal pressure for racial integration combined with urbanization and economic expansion to nurture the long-awaited two-party system that finally blossomed in the post-World War II South. As predicted, the Republican party attracted much of its support from an expanding bourgeoisie fed not only by upward mobility but by the in-migration of industrialists, entrepreneurs, and professionals. Political scientists such as V. O. Key hoped that southern economic development would create a legitimate two-party system based on a genuine division of class interests, rather than on the racial tensions that had helped to perpetuate the Democratic party's domination of southern politics. Presumably blacks would find themselves representing the balance of power between higher-income whites who flocked to the Republicans and lower-income whites who stayed in the Democratic camp. With the Democrats at last confronted with viable opposition, blacks would be able to win significant concessions in exchange for their support. The likely result seemed to be the long-awaited "have nots" coalition of blue-collar whites and blacks.

The anticipated benefits of two-party politics failed to materialize in the short run. The racial tensions of the early 1960s, particularly the angry reactions of southern whites to the Kennedy and Johnson administrations' support for black equality, proved to be the major factor in the Republican party's runaway growth during the mid-1960s. The Republican "go hunting where the ducks are" approach amounted to a none-too-subtle appeal to discontented Democrats based on the tacit assurance of less enthusiastic enforcement of civil rights statutes and policies under a GOP administration. Motivated by racial animosities, many whites flocked to the GOP banner at the same time that large numbers of newly registered blacks joined the Democratic ranks. The "southern strategy" of the Republican party amounted to a virtual write-off of black voters, who had no choice but to cast their lot with the Democrats, whose white faithful proved not nearly so faithful once black candidates began running under the Democratic banner.

Both Tennessee and Georgia provided useful examples of the short-run conservative impact of the rise of the GOP in the South. The most fertile breeding ground of Republicanism in Tennessee was the western counties, where, inspired by a "New Guard" based in Memphis, young, upwardly mobile farmers, business, industrial, and professional leaders joined hands to rally support for Barry Goldwater, the GOP presidential candidate, in 1964. The only liberal contender in the 1966 Georgia Democratic gubernatorial primary, former Governor Ellis Arnall, fell by the wayside in a runoff with Lester Maddox, an axe-handle wielding segregationist whose refusal to serve blacks at his "Pickrick" restaurant in Atlanta had endeared him to working-class whites. His Republican opponent, textile heir Howard "Bo" Callaway, who was also a segregationist, albeit a less obstreperous one, enjoyed the allegiance of affluent whites in the state's metropolitan areas. Callaway's appeal rested squarely on laissez faire economics and a clear lack of enthusiasm for civil rights measures. One working-class white voter is alleged to have explained his decision to support Maddox over Callaway by admitting that both were "agin' the nigger" but contending that "Bo thinks everybody who makes less than $20,000 a year is a nigger!"

The South's new two-party system lacked the rabid demagoguery so much a part of the one-party past, but Republicanism also reinforced the frugality and hostility to social welfare programs already common among corporate- and planter-oriented Democratic political leaders in the region. Writing in 1949, V. O. Key noted that North Carolina's politics and government had been uncommonly "progressive" for a southern state, especially in the support of public services and facilities and the general absence of demagoguery.

Stressing the importance of an "economic oligarchy" in influencing policymaking, Key concluded that North Carolina's politicians had generally been "unblushingly and unapologetically in favor of sound, conservative government. Progressive, forward looking, yes, but always sound, always the kind of government liked by the big investor, the big employer." The influence of the economic oligarchy had produced a political/governmental system on the one hand supportive of improvements in highways, public health, and education, but on the other capable, in the middle of the Depression, of imposing a sales tax while lowering ad valorem levies.

The South's new Republicans favored the reforms and expanded services likely to please the members of the region's expanding middle class or serve the interests of businessmen and industrialists. On the other hand, they normally opposed changes in the tax structure likely to make it less regressive or more dependent on corporate revenues. Key credited the business community for the relatively enlightened climate in North Carolina, but a recent study has shown that Tarheel political moderates often found themselves in conflict with corporate representatives when it came to progressive tax reform or what Paul Luebke called "political action that smacked of populism and/or economic egalitarianism."

World War II set in motion a number of economic and political trends, but prior to the federal civil rights pressure of the 1960s there was little reason to conclude that the South's conservative social order was incompatible with its economic progress. By the 1970s the South was enjoying the benefits of well-publicized economic growth and extensive praise for its favorable business climate, but social and political change was hardly a regional priority. It was particularly ironic that, after decades of insistence that social and institutional progress was a prerequisite for industrial development, a 1980 business climate survey accorded Mississippi, hardly a bastion of progressivism, the distinction of having the nation's most attractive business climate. A year later, when the same survey asked respondents to consider educational factors, Mississippi, with the nation's weakest public school system, fell only to sixth place. Such surveys revealed that the political conservatism, antigovernmentalism, fiscal frugality, and hostility to organized labor so long a part of the South's overall image of backwardness were actually essential ingredients in the recipe for Sunbelt prosperity.

The tendency to equate advanced industrial capitalism with an open, democratic, progressive society stemmed from a certain degree of nationalism—pride in the fruits of the nation's economic and political development as symbolized by the Industrial North. This point of view assumed a relationship between a society's means of production and its social and political institutions, a mutually dependent relationship requiring that changes in one be accompanied by proportionate changes in the other. Theoretically, as the South moved toward economic parity with the rest of the nation, its social and political structure and the nature and quality of its institutions would keep pace. If, as Woodrow Wilson and several decades of his disciples insisted, capitalism could be counted on to spread political and social progress abroad, could any less be expected of it within the borders of the United States?

Such reasoning rested on an historical misinterpretation of the goals and actions of American corporate leaders. For example, the social and political upheaval accompanying the late nineteenth-century economic revolution in the United States had been anything but comforting to many businessmen, industrialists, and professionals, some of whom took steps to nip rambunctious pluralism in the bud, especially where labor unions and lower-class political activism were concerned. The response of corporate America to the Populist movement was particularly telling on this point. Wall Street grew apoplectic at the prospect of democratized policymaking, more equitable taxation, and greater government regulation aimed at maintaining economic competition. Only after the Populists had been crushed did economic leaders embrace the stabilizing reforms of the Progressive era, which, despite their humanitarian contributions, also included a number of measures that further insulated the electoral and governmental process from pressures from below.

Corporate and industrial America has exhibited a decided apprehension about grassroots democracy not only at home but abroad as well. Lawrence Goodwyn noted this connection when he observed that "the popular aspirations of the people of the 'third world' in the twentieth century have easily become as threatening to modern Americans as the revolt of their own farmers was to gold bugs eighty years ago. . . . American foreign policy and American weapons have defended anachronistic feudal and military hierarchies in South America, Africa, and Asia, such actions being justified at home as necessary to the defense of 'democracy.'" Although not unconcerned with human uplift, in both their foreign and their domestic ventures, American investors have often placed greater emphasis on social and political stability than on equality of opportunity, citizen participation, public services and facilities, and assistance for the disadvantaged. In the industrializing South the potential for destabilization was greatly diminished by the energetic efforts of southern industrialists and development leaders to maintain the continuity that the growth of industry threatened to disrupt.

Many of the characteristics viewed by scholars as positive attributes of the Industrial North—worker activism, competition for labor, extensive social welfare programs, and significant government regulation—had been tolerable to the region's economic leaders largely because as a "core" area it was growing rapidly enough to provide consistently expanding profits, salaries, and wages and still meet the fiscal demands of government in a support and service society. Ironically, this society was financed to some extent by an advantageous relationship with the South, a peripheral area forced to share its economic pie with investors and financiers in the northern core. As operating efficiency decreased and overall costs mounted, locational and business climate surveys made it clear that many of the conditions that had made northern industrial society seem enlightened and progressive had actually contributed to decisions by corporate executives to forgo future investments and expansions in the North. Why was it reasonable to expect that, as they transferred their operations to the South, industrial investors would insist on transplanting the social, political, and governmental conditions that had caused them to shun the North? On the contrary, the ability to avoid these conditions, to practice the "unfettered capitalism" alluded to by Harold Woodman, was a major attraction as far as many southern industrialists were concerned.

Industrialists who spurned such "fetters" as government regulation and labor activism also showed little inclination to acknowledge the responsibility for creating new jobs in areas where unemployment was high and skill levels low. Industrialization seemed to promise a chance for southern blacks to overcome the legacy of discrimination and repression that kept them at the bottom of the economic ladder, but many southbound firms deliberately avoided locations with large concentrations of blacks. In Atlanta, for example, many companies that made use of bustling Hartsfield International Airport shunned the blacker, south side of the city despite its proximity to the airport. Several industrial recruiters told a *New York Times* reporter that some executives refused to consider locations in counties where blacks made up more than 30 percent of the population. A spokesman for Amoco Fabrics explained that his company's preference for areas with relatively few blacks reflected a simple desire for efficient, uncomplicated operation: "The lower the concentration of minorities, the better we're able to perform and get a plant started up."

This critical assessment of the American industrial executive should be kept in perspective. At home and abroad American investors were at least as philanthropic and progressive as their counterparts elsewhere in the world, but they were answerable to a society that saw them as both agents of capitalist prosperity and champions of social and political enlightenment. Industrial leaders were expected to "do good" as they "did well," and they often succeeded on both counts. When they faced a choice between these two priorities, however, they more often than not chose to protect their company's interests by opposing tax reforms, expanded social welfare programs, increased government regulation, or other measures likely to cut into their profits and inhibit their operations. In some cases such actions may have been better capitalism than citizenship, but to expect industrial and business executives to subordinate the short-term economic interests of their companies to the long-term interests of their states or communities was to expect of them a sacrifice that American workers and consumers and the organizations that represented them were often equally quick to reject.

If the typical industrialist failed to become a major force for change in the South, what of the rest of Dixie's rapidly expanding bourgeoisie? By 1980 the South's white-collar class was growing at the rate of three to four hundred thousand a year and made up approximately 25 percent of the region's population. More affluent, better educated, less overtly racist, the new middle class had played an important role in moderating the region's social and political climate. Nonetheless, the impact of middle-class expansion on the South was hardly as explosive as had been predicted. The failure of the new middle class to revolutionize the region's sociocultural and political environment can be better understood by exploring the reasons why such a revolution was predicted in the first place. Although Leonard Reissman exaggerated the historic desire of the middle class for social and political change, particularly sweeping change, Reissman did acknowledge that a major motivation for the bourgeoisie to champion modification of the existing order was the need to win "added support from those at the bottom of the social hierarchy." According to Reissman, as in developing nations where the bourgeoisie often tried to ameliorate the conditions of the potentially restive peasants, the southern middle class might be expected to champion change in the interest of creating "as stable a social order as possible and as quickly as possible."

Although by the 1980s some political scientists saw signs of a working class coalition that promised to make southern politics more responsive to the needs of lower income voters of both races, the failure of such a coalition to emerge during the first decade and a half of two-party politics illustrated the continuing absence of pressure from below that had characterized the post-Reconstruction South. Disfranchisement, manipulation of lower-class white racial anxieties, and vigorous repression of labor activism left the South without an organized "under class" capable of forcing the creation of a more open, competitive society with services and institutions more attuned to its needs.

Liberal observers, both North and South, were continually frustrated by the reluctance of white southerners to behave in self-interested, class-conscious, "northern" fashion by joining in a color-blind labor coalition to press for better wages in the work place and more influence in the political arena. In fact, the characteristically slow pace of southern industrial growth and the traditional adherence of most industrialists to the caste system had made the dedication of white workers to the status quo eminently rational in the short run. Where, after all, was the incentive to jeopardize the creation of jobs in a labor-surplus economy or to increase the competition for these jobs by uniting with blacks or championing racial equality? The more rapid growth of the post-World War II period mitigated these antipopulist circumstances, but nearly a century of manipulated antagonism and disadvantageous labor market conditions could not be expected to disappear overnight.

Union leaders argued that decades of deprivation should be all the more reason for southern workers to engage in the collective militance needed to bring them abreast of their northern counterparts, but most southern laborers avoided this course. If anything, their acquaintance with low wages and undesirable working conditions had left them all the more grateful for their jobs, even though these jobs paid less than jobs in similar plants elsewhere. Even in the Sunbelt era southern workers continued to respond to the neopaternalism of antiunion employers such as Nissan Motors. Although one United Auto Workers leader told *Newsweek* that Nissan's desire to hire "hard working country people" really amounted to an attempt to employ "peasants," the company's guarantees of lifetime employment, its efforts to involve employees in management decisions, and its recreational and fitness programs drew 100,000 applications for 2,600 jobs at its Smyrna, Tennessee, plant. Union officials were perplexed at the attitude of one Nissan worker who insisted: "If the company treats the workers well . . . there's nothing a union can offer." Such assertions were particularly confounding in light of the fact that this worker could have earned a starting wage that was $2.50 per hour higher if he had been employed in a unionized automobile plant in the North.

In the absence of a lower-class challenge, the South's middle class was able to confine its agenda for change to those items most in line with its members' economic interests and personal concerns. Still, should not their values alone have impelled them to demand improvements in services, facilities, and institutions sufficient to bring them in line with those elsewhere in the nation? For years social scientists had insisted that members of the upper and middle classes were "future oriented" and thus always stood ready to sponsor whatever changes were necessary to insure continuing improvement in the overall quality of life in their cities and communities. At the end of the 1970s, with nearly one-fourth of the region's business leaders northern born, the progressive northern influence that had been seen as so crucial to the South's transformation should certainly have been felt. Yet, while services, facilities, and institutions appeared to be making significant progress, statistical quality-of-life surveys still put the South far behind the rest of the nation. How could so many well-educated, affluent, northern-born migrants choose to live in a region where poverty was still such a problem and public services and cultural and entertainment possibilities so limited? The resounding endorsements that these new southerners gave their states challenged the assumption that all enlightened Americans shared a set of values and preferences typically associated with the lifestyles of the northern urban bourgeoisie.

Southerners who remembered the incessant South-baiting of H. L. Mencken had the last laugh when the results of Merle Black's thirteen-state analysis of resident preferences were shown to correlate at -.76 with the index of "civilization" that Mencken had constructed in 1931 to damn Mississippi as "the worst American state" and anoint Massachusetts as the best. Ironically, Massachusetts residents showed the least satisfaction with their state of any of the thirteen groups analyzed by Black in 1975.

John Shelton Reed offered the following explanation of the results of the survey: "The kind of economics and politics that can make a state healthy, wealthy and wise—civilized as Mencken would have it—can have at least short-run effects that people experience as debits in the quality of life ledger. For example, New York spends twice as much per pupil on education as North Carolina. Score one for the quality of life in New York when those pupils finish school. But North Carolina's taxes are about half of New York's, per capita. Score—how much?—for the quality of life in North Carolina right now."

Reed explained the reluctance of both native and transplanted members of the southern middle class to tamper with the status quo by arguing that "a given individual can quite rationally be unwilling to trade a clear and present good thing for a distant and hypothetical benefit." While it made sense to want to live in New York, it was not necessarily less sensible to want to live in North Carolina, or perhaps even Mississippi, without trying to transform them into New York. In the final analysis, many influential southerners had flown in the face of traditional scholarly wisdom by rejecting the short-term sacrifices necessary to achieve worthy but costly long-term societal goals.

Despite its deficiencies, statistical and otherwise, many intelligent, experienced Americans still managed to find much that was commendable about life in Dixie. If industrialization failed to cure all of the South's ills, it also failed to destroy many of its most appealing qualities. The Industrial North's long-playing role as the "state of the art" industrial society had left most social scientists, journalists, and liberal crusaders convinced that enlightened northerners, if forced to live in the South, would insist on remaking their new home in the image of their old one. Moreover, upwardly mobile native southerners were certain to cooperate by cosponsoring changes designed to revamp their region. The insistence of professional South-watchers that a more prosperous South must become a drawling version of the North resulted from a projection of their own values and prejudices on a population of executives, professionals, and workers who apparently saw life somewhat differently.

The failure of industrialization to induce greater social and political upheaval in the South may have been no more significant than the expectation that it would. This expectation reflected the extent to which the remarkable (and historically misunderstood) experience of the Industrial North had, in the minds of many Americans, become synonymous with the development of industrial capitalism regardless of the economic, cultural, or political context in which that development might occur. As American policymakers continue to intervene in the affairs of "developing" nations they would do well to study the example of the Industrial South, an example which raises some serious questions about their unfaltering conviction that economic modernization can guarantee sweeping human and institutional progress within any society.

The briefest glance at the South of 1984 with its skyscrapers, factories, and superhighways reveals that industrial development has brought significant changes to the region. Yet a closer analysis of contemporary conditions also shows that, for all its apparent impact, industrialization has not obliterated the socioeconomic and structural differences that have traditionally represented the fundamental basis of southern distinctiveness. Instead of witnessing a head-on collision between economic progress and deep-seated traditionalism, the post-Reconstruction South saw these two seemingly incompatible phenomena demonstrate a remarkable adaptability to each other. Welcomed by some and feared by others, industrialization actually served both as an agent of change and as a buttress for the status quo.

A new and truly complete perspective on the impact of industrialization on the South requires less emphasis on the region's resistance to change and more attention to the process of mutual adaptation between the influences of industrial expansion and the social, political, and cultural characteristics often associated with economic underdevelopment in Dixie. Expectations that the South's experience with industrialization would duplicate the North's ignored not only these characteristics but the structural differences between their respective economies at the time when industrialization began to accelerate in each. The historical circumstances that shaped the destiny of the agrarian South also played a major role in forging the character of an industrial South. Like the gloomy, defeated Dixie of 1877, the optimistic, skyscraper-studded Sunbelt South of the 1980s still reflected the influences of a complex heritage, a heritage whose best elements had recently become as difficult to preserve as its worst had been to overcome.

Bibliographic Note

General Studies and Resources

Despite increased interest in recent years, there is no overall history of southern industrial development. Emory Q. Hawk's *Economic History of the South* (New York: Prentice Hall, 1934) is helpful but dated. Thomas H. Naylor and James Clotfelter's *Strategies for Change in the South* (Chapel Hill: Univ. of North Carolina Press, 1975) presents only a brief survey of the stages of the region's economic/industrial growth as an introduction to a lengthy analysis of the South's needs and problems. More useful information is available in Susan Previant Lee and Peter Passell, *A New Economic View of American History* (New York: W.W. Norton, 1979). An excellent discussion of the need for more investigation of the economy of the post-Reconstruction South is Gerald D. Nash's "Research Opportunities in the Economic History of the South after 1880," *Journal of Southern History* 32 (Aug. 1966): 308-24.

In the absence of major analyses of southern industrial development, the reader may turn to several historical texts for information and insights. These include Clement Eaton, *A History of the Old South*, 4th ed. (New York: Alfred A. Knopf, 1972); John S. Ezell, *The South since 1865*, 2nd ed. (New York: Macmillan, 1975); C. Vann Woodward, *The Origins of the New South, 1877-1913* (Baton Rouge: Louisiana State Univ. Press, 1951); George B. Tindall, *The Emergence of the New South, 1913-1945* (Baton Rouge: Louisiana State Univ. Press, 1967); Idus A. Newby, *The South: A History* (New York: Holt Rinehart and Winston, 1978); and Charles P. Roland, *The Improbable Era: The South since World War II* (Lexington: Univ. Press of Kentucky, 1975).

Two particularly valuable state histories are Kenneth Coleman, ed., *A History of Georgia* (Athens: Univ. of Georgia Press, 1977); and Robert E. Corlew, *Tennessee: A Short History*, 2nd ed. (Knoxville: Univ. of Tennessee Press, 1981). David Goldfield's *Cotton Fields and Skyscrapers: Southern*

City and Region, 1607-1980 (Baton Rouge: Louisiana State Univ. Press, 1982) is helpful in clarifying the relationship between urbanization and industrialization. An important study of the "modernization" of a southern state is Numan V. Bartley's *The Creation of Modern Georgia* (Athens: Univ. of Georgia Press, 1983).

The best source of statistical data concerning southern industrial development is E. S. Lee, A. R. Miller, C. P. Brainerd, and R. A. Easterlin, *Population Redistribution and Economic Growth: United States, 1870-1950* (Philadelphia: American Philosophical Society, 1957). *The Statistical Abstract of the United States* and the *Census of Manufacturers* are also useful here. Since its inception in 1882 *The Manufacturer's Record* (which became *Industrial Development and Manufacturer's Record* in 1958 and *Industrial Development* in 1976) has provided numerous examples of southern industrial progress.

The Antebellum South

In *A Deplorable Scarcity: The Failure of Industrialization in the Slave Economy* (Chapel Hill: Univ. of North Carolina Press, 1981), Fred Bateman and Thomas Weiss present the most recent synthesis of scholarship and argument concerning the failure of the antebellum South to develop a more extensive manufacturing sector. They also provide an excellent up-to-date selected bibliography concerning industry in the Old South. Douglas C. North offers a brief analysis of the antebellum South's economy in *The Economic Growth of the United States, 1790 to 1860* (Englewood Cliffs, N.J.: Prentice Hall, 1961).

Studies of individual industries in the antebellum South include: Kathleen Bruce, *Virginia Iron Manufacturers in the Slave Era* (New York: A.M. Kelly, 1931); Ernest Lander, *The Textile Industry in Antebellum South Carolina* (Baton Rouge: Louisiana State University Press, 1967); John H. Moore, "Mississippi's Antebellum Textile Industry," *Journal of Mississippi History* 16 (Apr. 1954): 81-98; Randall Miller, "The Cotton Mill Movement in Antebellum Alabama" (Ph.D. diss., Ohio State Univ., 1971); Charles Kuhlmann, *The Development of the Flour Milling Industry in the U.S.* (Boston: Houghton Mifflin, 1929); and Joseph Roberts, *The Tobacco Kingdom* (Durham: Duke Univ. Press, 1938).

Broadus Mitchell's *William Gregg, Factory Master of the Old South* (Chapel Hill: Univ. of North Carolina Press, 1928) is a study of the Old South's premier textile industrialist. Charles B. Dew's *Ironmaker to the Confederacy: Joseph R. Anderson and the Tredegar Iron Works* (New Haven: Yale Univ. Press, 1966) looks at the manager of the antebellum South's most important "heavy" industry. Robert S. Starobin's *Industrial Slavery in the*

Old South (New York: Oxford Univ. Press, 1970) remains the major work on the role of slaves as industrial workers.

The estimates of Richard A. Easterlin in "Regional Income Trends, 1840-1950" in Seymour E. Harris, ed., *American Economic History* (New York: McGraw-Hill, 1961), and of Lee Soltow in *Men and Wealth in the United States, 1850-1870* (New Haven: Yale Univ. Press, 1975) challenge contentions that slavery impoverished the South and thereby made industrialization less likely. Thomas Weiss shows that profits in southern manufacturing occasionally exceeded the national average and greatly surpassed the profits typically accruing to a planter, in "Southern Business Never Had It So Good: A Look at Antebellum Industrialization" in Fred Bateman, ed., *Business in the New South: A Historical Perspective* (Sewanee, Tenn: Univ. Press, University of the South), pp. 27-34.

The Industrial Development Effort

Evidence on efforts to promote industrial development in the antebellum South may be found in Herbert Collins, "The Southern Industrial Gospel before 1860," *Journal of Southern History* 12 (Aug. 1946): 386-402; and Robert S. Cotterill, "The Old South to the New," *Journal of Southern History* 15 (Feb. 1949): 3-8.

Information on nineteenth-century urban boosterism is available in Goldfield, *Cotton Fields and Skyscrapers* (see above, pp. 165-66). A good case study is Sarah McCulloch Lemmon, "Raleigh—An Example of the New South," *North Carolina Historical Review* 43 (Summer 1966): 261-83. The mill building crusade in South Carolina is described in David L. Carlton, *Mill and Town in South Carolina, 1880-1920* (Baton Rouge: Louisiana State Univ. Press, 1982).

Henry W. Grady's *The New South and Other Addresses* (New York: Maynard Merrill, 1904) provides an opportunity to examine the rhetoric of the New South movement's premier orator. Raymond B. Nixon's *Henry W. Grady: Spokesman of the New South* (New York: Alfred A. Knopf, 1943) is a full-length biography. The standard work on the New South crusade is Paul M. Gaston, *The New South Creed: A Study in Southern Mythmaking* (New York: Alfred A. Knopf, 1970). Gaston and Vann Woodward see the New South movement representing the interests of an emergent commercial middle class. In his *Mind of the South* (New York: Alfred A. Knopf, 1941), Wilbur J. Cash argues that the crusade for "progress" actually helped to preserve and extend planter influence. Two relatively recent studies that generally support Cash's observations are Jonathan M. Wiener's *Social Origins of the New South: Alabama, 1860-1885* (Baton Rouge: Louisiana State Univ. Press, 1978); and Dwight B. Billings, Jr.'s *Planters and the Making of a New South: Class, Politics, and Development in North Carolina, 1865-1900* (Chapel Hill: Univ. of North Carolina Press, 1979). A provocative study of Mississippi during this period is Lester M. Salamon, "Protest, Politics, and Modernization in the American South: Mississippi as a 'Developing Society'" (Ph.D. diss., Harvard Univ., 1971). Wiener's article "Class Structure and Economic Development in the American South," *American Historical Review* 84 (Oct. 1979): 970-93, is also helpful.

A thorough review of the literature on southern progressivism is Dewey W. Grantham's "The Contours of Southern Progressivism," *American Historical Review* 86 (Dec. 1981): 1035-59. An excellent study identifying some of the differences between urban and rural progressivism is Jack Temple Kirby's *Darkness at the Dawning: Race and Reform in the Progressive South* (Philadelphia: J.B. Lippincott, 1972). A thorough state-level study is Charles G. Hamilton, "Mississippi Politics in the Progressive Era, 1904-1920" (Ph.D. diss., Vanderbilt Univ., 1958).

For an analysis that emphasizes the commitment of early twentieth-century Progressives to the New South development ideal, see J. Morgan Kousser, *The Shaping of Southern Politics: Suffrage Restriction and the Establishment of the One-Party South, 1880-1910* (New Haven: Yale Univ. Press, 1974), pp. 229-37. See also George B. Tindall, "Business Progressivism: Southern Politics in the Twenties," *South Atlantic Quarterly* 62 (Winter 1963): 92-106. Southern boosters of the 1920s evidenced a fervent belief in the New South Creed; see Blaine A. Brownell, *The Urban Ethos in the South, 1920-1930* (Baton Rouge: Louisiana State Univ. Press, 1975); and Charles P. Garofalo, "The Sons of Henry Grady: Atlanta Boosters in the 1920s," *Journal of Southern History* 62 (May 1976): 187-204.

For an examination of the emergence of state-sponsored industrial development efforts see William D. Ross, "Industrial Promotion by Southern States" (Ph.D. diss., Duke Univ., 1951); and Albert LePawsky, *State Planning and Economic Development in the South* (Kingsport, Tenn.: Kingsport Press, 1949). For a study of a community-based promotional program see Ernest J. Hopkins, *The Louisville Industrial Foundation: A Study in Community Capitalization of Local Industries* (Atlanta: Federal Reserve Bank of Atlanta, 1945).

Ernest J. Hopkins, *Mississippi's BAWI Plan: An Experiment in Industrial Subsidization* (Atlanta: Federal Reserve Bank of Atlanta, 1944) is a thorough analysis of the early BAWI program. The entire program is surveyed in Jack Edward Prince, "History and Development of the Mississippi Balance Agriculture with Industry Program, 1936-1958" (Ph.D. diss., Ohio State Univ., 1961). For an analysis of the effectiveness of tax exemptions in attracting new industry see William Edward Morgan, "The Effects of State and Local

Tax and Financial Inducements on Industrial Location" (Ph.D. diss., Univ. of Colorado, 1964).

Two articles that help to explain the relationship between changes in southern agriculture and the expanded crusade for industry are: Pete Daniel, "The Transformation of the Rural South, 1930 to the Present," *Agricultural History* 55 (July 1981): 231-48; and Numan V. Bartley, "Another New South," *Georgia Historical Quarterly* 65 (Summer 1981): 119-37.

For critical views of the practice of subsidization see American Federation of Labor, *Subsidized Industrial Migration: The Luring of Plants to New Locations* (Washington, D.C., n.p., 1955); "The Economic Consequences of BAWI," *Business Week*, Apr. 26, 1952; and John O. Garwood, "Are Municipal Subsidies for Industrial Location Sound?" *American City* 48 (May 1953): 110-11. A more favorable appraisal of subsidies may be found in John E. Moes, *Local Subsidies for Industry* (Chapel Hill: Univ. of North Carolina Press, 1962). See also "'Buy Industry' or 'You May Not Get It,' Says Lafayette Mayor Who Learned the Hard Way," *Tennessee Town and City* 8 (July 1957), 6:46. Examples of state and local subsidization of industry and of the intensity of the overall development effort may be found in the records and correspondence of state development agencies and the relevant correspondence of southern governors. Especially rich material is available in the North Carolina State Archives in Raleigh, the South Carolina State Archives in Columbia, and the Virginia State Archives in Richmond. Newspaper clipping files in state university libraries are also useful in this subject area. *Fortune, Business Week*, and other similar magazines provide numerous examples of the southern "sales pitch" to new industry as seen through development ads. The entire organized state and local development effort since the Great Depression is discussed extensively in James C. Cobb, *The Selling of the South: The Southern Crusade for Industrial Development, 1936-1980* (Baton Rouge: Louisiana State Univ. Press, 1982).

The most coherent critique of the South's pursuit of industry appeared in Twelve Southerners, *I'll Take My Stand: The South and the Agrarian Tradition* (New York: Harper Brothers, 1930). For the attitudes of southern literary figures toward the crusade for industrial development see Wayne Mixon, *Southern Writers and the New South Movement, 1865-1913* (Chapel Hill: Univ. of North Carolina Press, 1980). The Agrarian position is criticized in Clarence Cason, *90° in the Shade* (Chapel Hill: Univ. of North Carolina Press, 1935); and Henry L. Mencken, "Uprising in the Confederacy," *American Mercury* (Mar. 1931), pp. 380-81.

Late Nineteenth- and Early Twentieth-Century Industrial Development

Much of the literature dealing with this period is discussed in Harold D. Woodman's "Sequel to Slavery: The New History Views the Post Bellum South," *Journal of Southern History* 43 (Nov. 1977): 523-54. Peter Temin summarizes the various interpretations of the impact of the Civil War on southern economic development in "The Post-Bellum Recovery of the South and the Cost of the Civil War," *Journal of Economic History* 36 (Dec. 1976): 898-907.

In *One Kind of Freedom: The Economic Consequences of Emancipation* (London: Cambridge Univ. Press, 1977) Roger L. Ransom and Richard Sutch contend that southern manufacturing rebounded from the Civil War more readily than did agriculture. Ransom and Sutch suggest that the disappointing pace of southern economic growth in the late nineteenth century was attributable in large part to the poor performance of the region's agriculture rather than its industry, which grew relatively rapidly but from such a small initial base that the impact of its growth was far from sufficient to provide dramatic improvements in the region's economic condition.

In *The Political Economy of the Cotton South: Households, Markets and Wealth in the Nineteenth Century* (New York: W.W. Norton, 1978) Gavin Wright argues that the end of the antebellum cotton boom was at least as devastating to the South's economy as the Civil War. Wright also observes that by the end of the cotton boom the South's economy was all but locked into a pattern of growth based on low-wage, labor- and resource-exploitive industry. The structural factors that shaped southern growth are also discussed in William N. Parker, "The South in the National Economy, 1865-1970," *Southern Economic Journal* 46 (Apr. 1980): 1019-48.

For an analysis of southern industrial growth written from the perspective of the 1920s see Broadus Mitchell and George S. Mitchell, *The Industrial Revolution in the South* (Baltimore: Johns Hopkins Univ. Press, 1930). On the cotton textile industry see Broadus Mitchell, *The Rise of the Cotton Mills in the South* (Baltimore: Johns Hopkins Univ. Press, 1921); Jack Blicksilver, *Cotton Manufacturing in the Southeast: An Historical Analysis* (Atlanta: Bureau of Business and Economic Research, School of Business Administration, Georgia State College of Business Administration, 1959); and Mary J. Oates, *The Role of Cotton Textile Industry in the Economic Development of the Southeast, 1900-1940* (New York: Arno Press, 1975).

David Carlton's *Mill and Town in South Carolina, 1880-1920,* (see above, p. 167) explains the tensions induced in South Carolina by the growth of the mill labor force. For a look at the Alabama iron industry, see Justin Fuller, "Boom Towns and Blast Furnaces: Town Promotion in Alabama, 1885-1893," *Alabama Review* 29 (Jan. 1976): 37-48. For the timber industry in Mississippi see Jo Dent Hodge, "The Lumber Industry in Laurel, Mississippi at the Turn of the Nineteenth Century," *Journal of Mississippi History* 35 (Nov. 1973): 361-79.

For assessments of the South's industrial economy on the eve of World War II, see Howard W. Odum, *Southern Regions* (Chapel Hill: Univ. of North Carolina Press, 1936); Harriet L. Herring, *Southern Industry and Regional Development* (Chapel Hill: Univ. of North Carolina Press, 1940); and Calvin B. Hoover and Benjamin U. Ratchford, *Economic Resources and Policies of the South* (New York: Macmillan, 1951).

Southern Labor

The plight of the southern worker is outlined in the works of Tindall and Woodward (see above, p. 165). Woodward discusses the convict lease system in some detail. The standard work on peonage is Pete Daniel's *The Shadow of Slavery: Peonage in the South, 1901-1969* (New York: Oxford Univ. Press, 1973). Among the many studies of forced labor in the timber camps is Jerrell H. Shofner, "Forced Labor in the Florida Forests: 1880-1950," *Journal of Forest History* 25 (Jan. 1981): 14-25.

A better acquaintance with mill workers may be gained from John Kenneth Morland, *The Millways of Kent* (Chapel Hill: Univ. of North Carolina Press, 1958); Tom E. Terrill and Jerrold Hirsch, eds., *Such As Us: Southern Voices of the Thirties* (Chapel Hill: Univ. of North Carolina Press, 1978); and Dale Newman, "Work and Life in a Southern Textile Town," *Labor History* 19 (Spring 1978): 204-25. Wayne Flynt's *Dixie's Forgotten People: The South's Poor Whites* (Bloomington: Indiana Univ. Press, 1979) recounts the circumstances that kept poor whites poor, even in the age of industrialization.

Walter Davenport's "All Work and No Pay," *Colliers* 100 (Nov. 13, 1937): 9-10, 70-75, is an expose of the exploitation of southern workers, as is Thomas L. Stokes, *Carpetbaggers of Industry* (n.p.: Amalgamated Clothing Workers of America, 1937).

See also Glen Gilman, *Human Relations in the Industrial Southeast: A Study of the Textile Industry* (Chapel Hill: Univ. of North Carolina Press, 1955). On the persistence of regional wage differentials see Joseph Block, "Regional Wage Differentials, 1907-1946," *Monthly Labor Review* 66 (Apr. 1948): 371-77; and Victor R. Fuchs and Richard Perlman, "Recent Trends in Southern Wage Differentials," *Review of Economics and Statistics* 42 (Aug. 1960): 292-300. In "Measuring Union-Nonunion Earning Differences," *Monthly Labor Review* 97 (Dec. 1974): 3-9, Paul M. Ryscavage shows that nonunion workers earned significantly lower wages. On blacks in southern industry see Herbert R. Northup and Richard L. Rowan, *Negro Employ-*

ment in Southern Industry (Philadelphia: Univ. of Pennsylvania Press, 1970); James M. Stepp, "Comments," in Ernest M. Lander, Jr., and Richard J. Calhoun, eds., *Two Decades of Change: The South since the Supreme Court Desegregation Decision* (Columbia: Univ. of South Carolina Press, 1975), p. 54; Donald Dewey, "Negro Employment in Southern Industry," *Journal of Political Economy* 60 (Aug. 1952): 274-93; and Sheridan Maitland and James Cowhig, "Research on the Effects of Industrialization in Rural Areas," *Monthly Labor Review* 81 (Oct. 1958): 1121-24. See also Larry Wayne Shiffler, "Negro Participation in Manufacturing: A Geographical Appraisal of North Carolina" (M.A. thesis, Univ. of North Carolina, 1965).

The efforts of organized labor to gain a foothold in the South are discussed in the works of Woodward and Tindall (see above, p. 165). The best overall survey of organized labor in the South is F. Ray Marshall's *Labor in the South* (Cambridge: Harvard Univ. Press, 1967). Also helpful are Melton A. McLaurin, *Paternalism and Protest: Southern Cotton Mill Workers and Organized Labor, 1875-1905* (Westport, Conn.: Greenwood, 1971); and Phillip Taft, *Organizing Dixie: Alabama Workers in the Industrial Era*, rev. and ed. by Gary M. Fink (Westport, Conn.: Greenwood, 1981). The best account of the famous Gastonia textile strike is Liston Pope, *Millhands and Preachers: A Study of Gastonia* (New Haven: Yale Univ. Press, 1942); but Dan McCurry and Carolyn Ashbaugh, "Gastonia, 1929: Strike at the Loray Mill," *Southern Exposure* 6 (Winter 1974): 185-203, is also helpful.

Resistance to unionization is explored in Charles H. Martin, "Southern Labor Relations in Transition: Gadsden, Alabama, 1930-1943," *Journal of Southern History* 47 (Nov. 1981): 545-68; David Montgomery, "Violence and the Struggle for Unions in the South, 1880-1930," in Merle Black and John Shelton Reed, eds., *Perspectives on the American South: An Annual Review of Society, Politics and Culture* 1 (London: Gordon and Breach, 1980); John Ray Skates, Jr., "Fred Sullens (1877-1957) and the Growth of Organized Labor," *Southern Quarterly* 10 (Summer 1972): 341-51; and Billy H. Wyche, "Southern Industrialists View Organized Labor in the New Deal Years, 1933-1941," *Southern Studies* 19 (Summer 1980): 157-71. Organized labor's most famous adversary in the South is analyzed in J. Gary DiNunno, "J.P. Stevens: Anatomy of an Outlaw," AFL-CIO, *American Federationist* 83 (Apr. 1976): 1-8.

Lucy Randolph Mason's *To Win These Rights: A Personal Story of the CIO in the South* (Westport, Conn.: Greenwood, 1970) is an excellent "insider's" account of union organizing efforts in the South. *Southern Exposure* has provided many worker accounts of union-management clashes in the South; see especially the issue entitled "Here Come a Wind: Labor on the Move," 4 (Spring 1976), which contains an extensive labor history bibliography.

Impact of Industrialization

The overall impact of industrialization on the South Carolina Piedmont is detailed in Anthony M. Tang, *Economic Development in the Southern Piedmont, 1860-1950* (Chapel Hill: Univ. of North Carolina Press, 1958). In addition to the Maitland and Cowhig report (see above, p. 172), case studies of the effects of industrialization on selected areas abound in the form of government reports as well as Ph.D. dissertations and masters theses. For example, see: Arkansas Department of Labor, Employment Security Division, "The Effect of Industry on a Small Rural Community," mimeographed; Alexander H. Morrison, "The Impact of Industry on a Rural Area: A Case Study of Development in Warren and Surrounding Counties, 1930-1945 (Ph.D. diss., Univ. of Virginia, 1958); Neal Gambill Lineback, "Industrialization of a Rural Appalachian County: Alleghany County, North Carolina" (M.S. thesis, Univ. of Tennessee, 1967); and Charles McCarthur Wilson, "The Impact of Industrial Development on Lawrence County, Tennessee" (M.A. thesis, Univ. of Tennessee, 1965). Richard L. Simpson and David R. Norsworthy present an interesting analysis of industrialization in the Burlington-Graham, North Carolina, area in "Occupational Structure," in John C. McKinney and Edgar T. Thompson, eds., *The South in Continuity and Change* (Durham: Duke Univ. Press, 1965).

An interesting study which concludes that industrialization was not always an economic godsend is George I. Wilbur and Sheridan T. Maitland, *Industrialization in Chickasaw County, Mississippi: A Study of Rural Residents*, (Mississippi State Univ. Agricultural Experiment Station, Bulletin #652 January 1963). On the tendency for single employers to dominate small-town or rural areas see Ralph R. Triplette, "One Industry Towns: Their Location, Development, and Economic Character" (Ph.D. diss., Univ. of North Carolina, 1974); and Bernice Larson Webb, "Company Town—Louisiana Style," *Louisiana History* 4 (Fall 1968): 325-38.

Ronald D. Eller takes a new look at the concept of "progress" in *Miners, Millhands and Mountaineers: The Modernization of the Appalachian South* (Knoxville: Univ. of Tennessee Press, 1982). A personal account of the effects of industrialization on life in the rural South is Ben Robertson's *Red Hills and Cotton: An Upcountry Memory* (New York: Alfred A. Knopf, 1942).

Industrial Development and Social and Political Change

For the classic statement of the relationship between social and political progress and economic growth see William H. Nicholls, *Southern Tradition and Regional Progress* (Chapel Hill: Univ. of North Carolina Press, 1960).

Leonard Reissman also put great faith in industrialization because it would give the South its long-awaited middle class; see his "Social Development and the American South," *Journal of Social Issues* 22 (Jan. 1966): 101-16. A similar point of view appears in John C. McKinney and Linda Brookover Bourque, "The Changing South: National Incorporation of a Region," *American Sociological Review* 35 (June 1971): 399-412. Those who expected urbanization to transform the South relied on a model described in Louis Wirth, "Urbanism as a Way of Life," *American Journal of Sociology* 74 (July 1938): 1-24. Those who used this model assumed that the South's cities would become classic "industrial" cities, but most manufacturing plants were located in small towns. See Richard E. Lonsdale and Clyde E. Browning, "Rural-Urban Locational Preferences of Southern Manufacturers," *Annals of the Association of American Geographers* 61 (June 1971): 255-68. The failure of urbanization to transform the South is discussed in James C. Cobb, "Urbanization and the Changing South: A Review of Literature," *South Atlantic Urban Studies* 1 (1977): 253-66.

J. Milton Yinger and George E. Simpson linked industrialization to the destruction of caste in "Can Segregation Survive in an Industrial Society?" *Antioch Review* 28 (Mar. 1958): 15-24. James W. Silver expressed a similar view in *Mississippi: The Closed Society* (New York: Harcourt, Brace and World, 1963). Ralph McGill described the conservative power structure of the small-town South in *The South and Southerners* (Boston: Little, Brown, 1964). William D. Barnard provides insight into the role of businessmen and industrialists in the Dixiecrat movement in *Dixiecrats and Democrats: Alabama Politics, 1942-1950* (University: Univ. of Alabama Press, 1974).

On the role of businessmen and industrialists in the early days of the civil rights movement see Numan V. Bartley, *The Rise of Massive Resistance: Race and Politics in the South during the 1950s* (Baton Rouge: Louisiana State Univ. Press, 1969). See also Neil R. McMillen, *The Citizen's Council: Organized Resistance to the Second Reconstruction* (Urbana: Univ. of Illinois Press, 1971). Earl Black, *Southern Governors and Civil Rights: Racial Segregation as a Campaign Issue in the Second Reconstruction* (Cambridge: Harvard Univ. Press, 1976), emphasizes the moderating influence of businessmen; while M. Richard Cramer, "School Desegregation and New Industry: The Southern Community Leader's Viewpoint," *Social Forces* 41 (May 1963): 384-89, shows the limits of that moderation. See Ronald E. Carrier and William R. Schriver, *Plant Location Analysis: An Investigation of Plant Locations in Tennessee* (Memphis: Memphis State Univ. Press, 1960), for a polling of industrialists regarding their concerns about the civil rights reputation of potential locations.

The Anti-Defamation League of B'nai B'rith, tried to use the "economic angle" to promote desegregation in *The High Cost of Conflict: A Roundup* of Opinion from the Southern Business Community on the Economic Consequences of School Closings and Violence (n.p., n.d.). Lorin A. Thompson did the same in "Virginia Education Crisis and Its Economic Aspects," *New South* 14 (Feb. 1959): 3-9. The "Southern Leadership Project" files at the Southern Regional Council in Atlanta are helpful on this subject, as are the gubernatorial papers of J. Lindsay Almond, Jr., in the Virginia State Archives, Richmond; Luther H. Hodges in the North Carolina State Archives, Raleigh; and George C. Wallace in the Alabama State Archives, Montgomery. A major source of information about perceptions of the economic impact of the desegregation crisis is the Southern Educational Reporting Service Clipping File, available on microfilm at a number of libraries, including the University of Georgia Library, Athens. The role of businessmen in the Montgomery crisis is discussed by J. Mills Thornton III, in "Challenge and Response in the Montgomery Bus Boycott of 1955-56," *Alabama Review* 32 (July 1980): 163-235. The failure of the economic elite of New Orleans to provide moderate leadership during that city's desegregation crisis is explored in Edward F. Haas, *DeLesseps S. Morrison and the Image of Reform: New Orleans Politics, 1946-1961* (Baton Rouge: Louisiana State Univ. Press, 1974). In *Mississippi: The Long Hot Summer* (New York: W.W. Norton, 1965) William McCord briefly discusses the behavior of that state's businessmen during the civil rights movement. A valuable collection of essays dealing with the economic community's response to desegregation in several southern cities, including Atlanta, Little Rock, Birmingham, Dallas, and Tampa, is Elizabeth Jacoway and David R. Colburn, eds., *Southern Businessmen and Desegregation* (Baton Rouge: Louisiana State Univ. Press, 1982).

In *Southern Politics in State and Nation* (New York: Vintage Books, 1949) V. O. Key, Jr., discusses industrial development as an influence for moderation and bipartisanship. The rise of Republicanism and its short-run conservative impact are explained in Numan V. Bartley and Hugh D. Graham, *Southern Politics and the Second Reconstruction* (Baltimore: Johns Hopkins Univ. Press, 1975); and Norman L. Parks, "Tennessee Politics since Kefauver and Reece: A Generalist View," *Journal of Politics* 28 (Feb. 1966): 144-68. Paul Luebke presents an analysis of corporate conservatism in "Corporate Conservatism and Government Moderation in North Carolina," in John Shelton Reed and Merle Black, eds., *Perspectives on the American South: An Annual Review of Society, Politics and Culture* 1 (London: Gordon and Breach, 1981): 107-18. Lawrence Goodwyn analyzes antipopulist sentiment among businessmen and industrialists in *Democratic Promise: The Populist Moment in America* (New York: Oxford Univ. Press, 1976).

For examinations of the antipopulist tendencies of southern workers see Richard H. King's discussion of the work of V. O. Key in *A Southern*

Renaissance: The Cultural Awakening of the American South, 1930-1955 (New York: Oxford Univ. Press, 1980), pp. 249-56; and Robert E. Botsch *We Shall Not Overcome: Populism and Southern Blue Collar Workers* (Chapel Hill: Univ. of North Carolina Press, 1980).

For examples of business and civic sponsorship of community improvement projects aimed at attracting new industry see "This Town Was Jilted," *Changing Times* 4 (Oct. 1950): 2; "You Gotta Have a Golf Course," *Business Week*, June 25, 1955, pp. 86-87; and William D. Angel, Jr., "Zenith Revisited: Urban Entrepreneurship and the Sunbelt Frontier," *Social Science Quarterly* 61 (Dec. 1980):434-45.

On the relationship between the quality of public schools and industrial development see Paul A. Montello, "The Importance of Educational Factors in Industrial and Business Site Selection," in Dick Howard, ed., *Guide to Industrial Development* (Englewood Cliffs, N.J.: Prentice Hall, 1972), pp. 349-82.

Cameron Fincher stresses the importance of research facilities in "Research in the South: An Appraisal of Current Efforts," Georgia State College, School of Arts and Sciences, Research Paper no. 5, mimeographed (1964). One view of the Research Triangle appears in Luther H. Hodges, *Businessman in the Statehouse* (Chapel Hill: Univ. of North Carolina Press, 1962). The Hodges Correspondence in the North Carolina State Archives, Raleigh, provides valuable information on "behind-the-scenes" efforts to promote the Triangle.

The Rise of the Sunbelt South

Two contemporary accounts of the emergence of the Sunbelt are Kevin P. Phillips, *The Emerging Republican Majority* (New Rochelle, N.Y.: Arlington House, 1969); and Kirkpatrick Sale, *Power Shift: The Rise of the Southern Rim and Its Challenge to the Eastern Establishment* (New York: Random House, 1975). On the media's love affair with the Sunbelt see Gene Burd, "The Selling of the Sunbelt: Civic Boosterism in the Media" in David C. Perry and Alfred J. Watkins, eds., *Urban Affairs Annual Review* 14 (1977) (Beverly Hills: Sage, 1977). See also Larry L. King, "We Ain't Trash No More," *Esquire* 126 (Nov. 1976): 89-90, 152-56. For a more penetrating analysis of changing perceptions of the South see C. Vann Woodward, "The South Tomorrow," *Time* Sept. 27, 1976, pp. 98-99; and Jack Temple Kirby, *Media-Made Dixie: The South in the American Imagination* (Baton Rouge: Louisiana State Univ. Press, 1978). On attracting foreign industry to the South see "Recruiting Industry Abroad," *South* 5 (Apr. 1978): 31-32.

On the efforts of twentieth-century observers to understand the South's economic development see Clarance H. Danhof, "Four Decades of Thought on the South's Economic Problems," in Melvin L. Greenhut and W. Tate

Whitman, *Essays in Southern Economic Development* (Chapel Hill: Univ. of North Carolina Press, 1964). A valuable economic analysis of the rise of the Sunbelt appears in Bernard L. Weinstein and Robert E. Firestine, *Regional Growth and Decline in the United States: The Rise of the Sunbelt and the Decline of the Northeast* (New York: Praeger, 1978). Weinstein and Firestine summarize several theories of regional growth, including those of Joseph Schumpeter presented in *The Theory of Economic Development* (Cambridge: Harvard Univ. Press, 1934); *Business Cycles* (New York: McGraw-Hill, 1939); and *Capitalism, Socialism, and Democracy* (New York: Harper and Brothers, 1947). See also Blaine Liner and Lawrence K. Lynch, eds., *The Economics of Southern Growth* (Durham, N.C.: Seeman, 1977). On regional economic convergence see Max Moise Schreiber, "The Development of the Southern United States: A Test for Regional Convergence and Homogeneity" (Ph.D. diss., Univ. of South Carolina, 1978). Immanuel Wallerstein provides an excellent comparative perspective for studying the South's development as a region in *The Modern World System: Capitalist Agriculture and the Origins of the European World Economy in the Sixteenth Century* (New York: Academic Press, 1974), vol. 1.

Joe Persky provides important clarification of the South's "colonial" status in "The South: A Colony at Home," *Southern Exposure* 1 (Summer/Fall 1973): 15-22. In the same issue of *Southern Exposure* see "Southern Militarism," "State Profiles," and "Charts" (60-62, 63-93, 94-99) for evidence of the Sunbelt South's "defense dependency."

The most cogent argument that the South's economic ascendancy was based on an inequitable distribution of federal funds appeared in "Federal Spending: The North's Loss Is the Sunbelt's Gain," *National Journal* 8 (June 26, 1976): 878-91. In *A Myth in the Making: The Southern Economic Challenge and Northern Economic Decline* (Washington, D.C.: United States Department of Commerce, Economic Development Administration, 1976), Carol L. Jusenius and Larry C. Ledeber attempt to refute charges that the South has profited at the North's expense in the allocation of federal spending.

For a close analysis of the impact of industrial migration on regional economic growth see Peter M. Allaman and David L. Birch, "Components of Employment Change for States by Industry Group, 1970-72," Working Paper #5, Inter-Area Migration Project, Joint Center for Urban Studies of MIT and Harvard University, September 1975. See also Jeanne C. Biggar, "The Sunning of America: Migration to the Sunbelt," *Population Bulletin* 24, no. 1 (Washington, D.C.: Population Preference Bureau, 1979). James M. Howell explores the backgrounds of southern businessmen in "Shifting Patterns in Southern Business Leadership," *Review of Regional Economics and Business* 4 (Oct. 1979): 3-9.

The Sunbelt South: Problems and Prospects

Southern cultural persistence is persuasively and cogently discussed by John Shelton Reed in *The Enduring South: Subcultural Persistence in Mass Society* (Lexington, Mass.: D.C. Heath Lexington Books, 1971); and *One South: An Ethnic Approach to Regional Culture* (Baton Rouge: Louisiana State Univ. Press, 1982).

The question of the survival of the South as a distinctive region despite its economic growth is also discussed by Kirby in *Media-Made Dixie* (see above, p. 176); by John Egerton in *The Americanization of Dixie: The Southernization of America* (New York: Harper's Magazine Press, 1974); and by Joel Garreau, *The Nine Nations of North America* (Boston: Houghton Mifflin, 1981). See also Marshall Frady, "Gone with the Wind," *Newsweek*, July 28, 1975, p. 11.

Merle Black's findings in "Is North Carolina Really the 'Best' American State?" in Thad L. Beyle and Merle Black, eds., *Politics and Policy in North Carolina* (New York: MSS Publications, 1975), are in direct contrast to the view of the quality of life in the South presented in Charles Angoff and H. L. Mencken, "The Worst American State," *American Mercury* 24 (Sept., Oct., Nov. 1931): 1-16, 177-88, 355-71. The South's inability to make Henry Grady's dream a reality is discussed in Charles P. Roland, "The South, America's Will-o'-the-Wisp Eden," *Louisiana History* 11 (1970): 101-19.

For a skeptical assessment of the Sunbelt phenomenon see George B. Tindall, "The Sunbelt Snow Job," *Houston Review* (Spring 1979): 3-13. The persistence of poverty in the Sunbelt South is documented in Jusenius and Ledeber, *A Myth in the Making* (see above, p. 177); and in Brian Rungeling, Lewis H. Smith, Vernon M. Briggs, Jr., and John F. Adams, *Employment, Income and Welfare in the Rural South* (New York: Praeger, 1977). Emil Malizia sparked controversy with his critical analysis of North Carolina's industrial economy in "The Earnings of North Carolina Workers," *University of North Carolina Newsletter* 60 (Dec. 1975): 1-4. On the underutilization of taxation see Kenneth E. Quindry and Niles Schoening, *State and Local Tax Ability and Effort, 1977* (Atlanta: Southern Regional Education Board, 1979). On the conflict between recruiting better-paying industry and keeping out unions, see Cliff Sloan and Bob Hall, "It's Good to Be Home in Greenville . . . But It's Better If You Hate Unions," *Southern Exposure* 7 (Spring 1979): 83-93. *Time, Newsweek, U.S. News and World Report, The Economist*, the *Wall Street Journal* and the *New York Times* regularly report the South's continuing struggle against labor unions as well as the persistence of economic discrimination. For a look into the Sunbelt's future in a "post-industrial" economy see Barry Bluestone and Bennett Harrison, *The Deindustrialization of America: Plant Closings, Community Abandonment, and the Dismantling of Basic Industry* (New York: Basic Books, 1982).

Industrial Location

The literature on industrial location is voluminous and confusing. An often-cited survey that overstresses the market attraction of the post-World War II South is Glenn E. McClaughlin and Stefan Robock, *Why Industry Moves South: A Study of Factors Influencing the Recent Location of Manufacturing Plants in the South*, NPA Committee of the South, report no. 3 (Kingsport, Tenn.: Kingsport Press, 1949). Victor R. Fuchs emphasizes the importance of cheap labor in *Changes in the Location of Manufacturing in the United States since 1929* (New Haven: Yale Univ. Press, 1962).

A more recent attempt to pinpoint the major factors in industrial location decisions is Leonard F. Wheat's *Regional Growth and Industrial Location* (Lexington, Mass.: Lexington Books, 1973). The South's attraction for industry may be best explained by its ability to offer a combination of factors such as cheap labor, cooperative government, and low taxes, as well as a growing pool of consumers. Thus the overall "business climate" is of paramount importance. Several studies of business climates show the southern states with a distinct advantage in this area. See, for example, Alexander Grant and Company, *A Study of Manufacturing Business Climates of the Forty-eight Contiguous States of America, 1980* (prepared in cooperation with the Conference of State Manufacturers Associations). In this ranking of business climates, eleven of the top twenty states were located in the South.

Industrial Development and the Environment

Except for the effects of coal mining in Appalachia, relatively little attention has been given to the environmental impact of industrialization in the South. Harry M. Caudill's *Night Comes to the Cumberlands: A Biography of a Depressed Area* (Boston: Little Brown, 1963) is a moving depiction of the destruction of the Appalachian environment. See also James Branscom, "Paradise Lost," and John Gaventa, "In Appalachia: Property Is Theft," *Southern Exposure* 1 (Summer/Fall 1973): 29-41, 43-52. An excellent analysis of the careless exhaustion of Mississippi's timber resources is Nollie W. Hickman's "Mississippi Forests" in Richard Aubrey McLemore, *A History of Mississippi*, 2 vols. (Hattiesburg: College and Univ. Press of Mississippi, 1973) 2: 212-32. For a look at the thoughtless destruction of timber resources in early twentieth-century Louisiana see Anna C. Burns, "The Gulf Lumber Company, Fullerton: A View of Lumbering during Louisiana's Golden Era," *Louisiana History* 20 (Spring 1979): 197-207.

James M. Fallows, *The Water Lords* (New York: Grossman, 1971), is an exposé of industrially-induced water pollution. Leslie Allan, Eileen Kohl Kaufman, and Joanna Underwood discuss the pollution caused by some of the South's paper mills in *Paper Profits: Pollution in the Pulp Industry* (Cambridge: MIT Press, 1972). For an excellent case study of the conflict between economic need and environmental protection see Oliver G. Wood, Jr., et al., *The BASF Controversy: Employment vs. Environment*, Bureau of Business and Economic Research, University of South Carolina, Essays in Economics Series, no. 25 (Columbia: Univ. of South Carolina Press, 1971). On this same controversy see Marshall Frady, "A Question of Plastics in Beaufort County," in Marshall Frady, *Southerners: A Journalist's Odyssey* (New York: New American Library, 1980), pp. 286-302. Pollution of the Gulf Coast is discussed in Joseph A. Pratt, "Growth or a Clean Environment? Response to Petroleum-related Pollution in the Gulf Coast Refining Region," *Business History Review* 61 (Spring 1977): 1-29.

The South's love affair with the nuclear industry is described by J. Samuel Walker in "The South and Nuclear Energy, 1954-62," *Prologue* 13 (Fall 1981): 175-91. The environmental attitudes of residents of the South's most ardently pro-nuclear state are presented in Louis Harris and Associates, "Priorities for Progress in South Carolina," study no. 2130, mimeographed (Oct. 1971).

The *New York Times* and the *Wall Street Journal* provided thorough coverage of pollution law violations by industries during the 1970s. For the debate on the Clean Air Act Amendments see *Congressional Record*, 94th Congress, 2nd Session, vol. 122; and 95th Congress, 1st Session, vol. 123. For a discussion of the potential impact of Clean Air Act Amendments on industrial development see Carlton B. Scott, "Clean Air Act Amendments Loom as Threat to Industrial Expansion," *Industrial Development* 147 (July/Aug. 1978): 9-12.

Index